MW00720269

The Disappearance of Richard Swann

Mark Carlile

A Memoir

First Published in 2016 by Michael G. Coates, Publishing. British Columbia, Canada

Copyright © Michael G Coates 2016
All rights reserved. No part of this publication may be reproduced, stored in a retrieval system, or transmitted, in any form or by any means, electronic, mechanical, photocopying, recording, or otherwise, without the written prior permission of the author.

ISBN: 978-0-9937154-3-3

Printed by CreateSpace, an Amazon.com Company

Available from book stores, and online book retailers, including:

Amazon.com
Amazon Europe
Amazon.ca
CreateSpace Direct
CreateSpace eStore
Barnes & Noble
Ingram
NACSCORP

Available as an e-book at:

Amazon.com
Amazon Kindle Store

The Disappearance of Richard Swann

Mark Carlile

It was an idyllic childhood for two children growing up on a farm in the quiet, picturesque East Devon countryside. But the sudden disappearance of a neighbour, wealthy tea merchant and property owner Richard Swann, in 1947 created intrigue for the small community of Stockland. Where was Richard Swann? That was the question Scotland Yard tried to answer. Had he simply left his family for some other life? Or had something more sinister occurred? Mark Carlile looks back at the past and the mystery that surrounded an isolated cottage.

Author's notes

I have used the name Mark Carlile to maintain continuity with former and future books.

My father wrote a memoir of his life, but never managed to complete it. I have incorporated small parts of his memoir in this book.

My next book The Key to a Murder, a novel, is due out in the spring of 2017.

Contents

Dedication

This book is dedicated to my grandmother,
Mary Coates, and Aunty Dorothy.

Chapter 1

Evacuation

The Coates family lived in Fairlight, a coastal village in Sussex. It is situated five miles from the towns of Rye, Hastings and Battle. Fairlight is located near the area known as The Firehills, which forms part of Hastings Country Park with its 500 acres of cliff walks, unspoiled wooded countryside and magnificent coastal views. The parish church, built in 1845, has an 82-foot tower. The village is mentioned in records of 1220 as Fairlight. In the days of smuggling, contraband goods were landed at Fairlight and brought inland by a tunnel.

The Coates family lived in this idyllic village. Mary had three daughters: Dorothy, Nancy and Muriel, and a son Bernard. Her husband Arthur ran a grocery store. The three girls ran a riding stable and rode their horses through the Firehills, and along the cliff top paths of Fairlight Glenn. Bernard was a carpenter. He married Sylvia Vile in 1939. I was born in 1941. Sadly, my mother passed away from toxaemia just after I was born. When the Second World War with Germany broke out in 1939, my father joined the military service. He served with the British Forces in India and Europe as a military policeman. To escape bombing raids during the early part of the war, the Coates family evacuated to east Devon and purchased Cummings farm. Cummings farm is located in the county of Devon near the small village of Stockland, and only a short drive to the town of Axminster. East Devon is renowned for its picturesque countryside of rolling hills, grassy farmlands, meandering streams, rivers and creeks, wooded combes, and vast areas of heathland. Because of its scenic beauty, east Devon attracts many summer visitors who explore the narrow lanes, quiet country villages, coastal fishing villages, towns and beaches.

The family left not only a home, but also two businesses in a quaint and attractive part of Sussex. Although equally scenic as their beloved Sussex, it was a big upheaval and sacrifice to relocate to an unknown area. It meant the loss of the girls' businesses, and Arthur's job in the grocery shop.

The decision was not easy but was made for the safety of all the family which included myself, and my cousin Noreen, the daughter of Dorothy. Dorothy's husband Billy had joined the Royal Air Force. If their home had been bombed, they risked the loss of their investment in the property and faced the ultimate risk of being killed or badly injured. The decision had been made, and they moved in the spring of 1942.

The laneway to Cummings farm is long, narrow and rough, with potholes that fill with water when it rains. High hedgerows with an overgrowth of trees and bushes line both sides of the lane with the occasional break by a five-bar gate that leads into the entrance of a field. The laneway climbed up a gentle grade until it reached a large cobbled farmyard with the old stone farmhouse directly ahead. Opposite the farmhouse stood a large stone barn that was shelter for farm animals, farm implements and animal feed.

My memory of Cummings is very faint as I was only a four-year-old when the war ended. I can remember my Grandmother and me sitting up late one night in the kitchen, waiting for my father to come home from the war after he was demobbed from service. The spacious kitchen had a flagstone floor. An oil lamp sitting on the large wooden kitchen table was the only source of light.

I can remember walking with Noreen down the laneway to a dump on the side of the lane that contained an assortment of empty tin cans. Sometimes the cans would rattle when we disturbed a rat that was hiding in this assortment of refuse, and we would go running back up the lane to the safety of the farmyard.

On January 27, 1945, Aunt Muriel married a local farmer, Cecil Venn. At 10:45 in the morning, Cecil arrived at the vicar's home in Stockland with a message that they would have to delay the time of the wedding from 12 noon until 2 p.m. Deep snow in Cummings lane prevented the bride from arriving sooner. When Cecil crossed the courtyard in front of the vicar's home, the vicar noticed that the snow was up to the top of his Wellingtons. Because the roads were impassable due to the heavy snowfall, Muriel was driven to the church at Stockland in a horse-drawn cart.

The vicar would later record in his diary that "It was a truly charming village wedding, the sun shining in a world transformed to radiant whiteness. The bride in white was accompanied by bridesmaids in royal blue wearing warm cloaks. Friends and relatives came to church in a brightly painted red and blue wagon, drawn by two brown horses with Mr. Venn driving and Walter Loveridge riding postilion."

"It took the village back a hundred years," commented Tom Moore, a parishioner.

The family did not stay at Cummings for many years before moving to another farm called Snodwell, which was only a few miles away on the other side of Stockland.

The road from Stockland is very narrow as it climbs uphill and then dips down to the bridge over Corry Brook. We crossed the bridge in our car then climbed up another steep hill to the junction of a road known as Stockland Hill that was built by the Romans after their invasion in 43 AD. Stockland Hill runs across high

3

ground, and unlike most roads in England was straight for about three miles, which was typical of the roads constructed by the Romans so many years ago.

We turned right at the junction and after about two miles made a left turn at a narrow laneway called Post Lane. It ran straight and flat for about half a mile along the crest of the hill before dipping down steeply to the valley below. The land to our left was part of Post Farm, and was covered with yellow flowering prickly gorse, scrub grass and tall fern. Very little use for farming except for the grazing of cattle. The road was just wide enough for two cars to pass if the grass verge on each side of the road was used, but then narrowed to the width of only one vehicle. If two vehicles met, one would have to reverse back until a gateway was found that provided a little more space. Gateways were generally set back a few yards from the road. The laneway to Snodwell Farm was at the bottom of the hill. It was rough, potholed, and muddy when it rained, which was frequent during winter. Banks, hedges, and tall oak and fir trees were prominent in places. I can remember my grandfather being dived at by a sparrow hawk that was trying to protect its nest in a large tree. It happened as he walked along the lane to the farmhouse one evening at dusk. The lane ran for about a mile before entering into a cobbled yard surrounded by the farmhouse, livestock buildings and a large hay barn.

The farmhouse was an 'L' shaped building, built of stone with a slate tile roof. One part of the 'L' contained a dairy on the upper level with animal shelter below. When the house was built it was not uncommon to have animals contained in part of the farmhouse. I remember very little about the interior of the house. I can remember the kitchen with its large wooden table, flagstone floor and iron range for heating and cooking. It was at the back of the house overlooking the yard. I can remember a large Christmas tree in the corner of the sitting room that my father cut down just before

Christmas one year, and a big stone fireplace with a crackling wood fire.

I would have been about five and a half years old at the time. Before I turned five in September, Noreen and I started at the village school in Stockland, which was on June 3, 1946. That I remember very well. Stockland School was an old stone building with a steep gable roof that was built in 1859. It looked more like an old stone farmhouse rather than a school.

"You two kids are starting school on Monday," Dorothy said.

"I don't want to go to school," Noreen immediately replied. "I'm not going."

Noreen's fifth birthday was in February of that year. But Dorothy decided to keep her back until I started school, so that we could both start school together.

My Aunt Dorothy drove us to Stockland School in the black 1934 Rover car that belonged to my father. It had doors with hinges at the back, a spare wheel mounted just above the back bumper and big chrome headlights. Just above the polished wood dashboard a small handle could be turned to tilt out the bottom of the front windscreen for additional ventilation.

"I'm not going," Noreen said, as her mother opened the door for her to get into the back seat of the car on the Monday morning.

"Michael's going," she said. "You have to go with him."

"No, I'm not going," Noreen insisted, and wriggled free from her mother's grip, and ran back into the house.

Dorothy was starting to get annoyed with her as she brought Noreen back out to the car and quickly lifted her in and closed the door.

Noreen sat sullenly on the back seat and sulked all the way to Stockland. I sat quietly beside her staring out the side window, exhaling deep breaths against the window so that I could make patterns in the fogged-up glass with my finger.

Mark Carlile

When we arrived at the school, Dorothy parked the car on the road beside the school playground which was slightly elevated from the road. I got out of the car but Noreen curled up on the back seat and had decided that she was not going anywhere.

"Okay Noreen, you have to get out and go to school," her mother said to her.

"I'm not going," she replied. "I don't have to go if I don't want to."

"Yes you do, get out of the car. Now."

Noreen started to cry and refused to move. Her mother caught hold of her arm and shoulder and pulled her out of the car. Noreen tried to resist, but it was futile. She quickly realized her mother was much stronger and gave in. I climbed the two steps up to the playground followed by Dorothy, who was half dragging Noreen by the arm to get her up the steps to the playground. Noreen started to cry again with deep sobs and tears flooding down her cheeks. A teacher in the schoolyard who was monitoring the children noticed Noreen's resistance and came over to help.

"You go," she said to Dorothy. "I'll hold onto her while you drive away."

Noreen clung to her mother's leg with both arms and refused to let go.

"No, no, don't go," she screamed. "I don't want you to go. Please don't go."

"I have to go Noreen," she replied. "The teacher will stay with you."

The teacher freed her from her mother's leg and held her while her mother left the playground and made her way back to the car. Noreen was pulling and screaming and trying to break free from the teacher, but the teacher had a firm hold on her and did not let go. They were near the railings around the schoolyard and Noreen could see her mother getting into her car from the elevated playground. Noreen suddenly broke free from the teacher and made a lunge for the railings. She started yelling and screaming.

Evacuation

"Don't go Mummy, come back, please don't go, please." All the while, tears were streaming down her cheeks and her face was flushed red in anger.

Dorothy was upset about leaving her like this, but forced herself to ignore her daughter and quickly drove away.

After Dorothy left, the teacher bent down and wiped Noreen's eyes and tried to calm her down.

"Your mummy will be back to pick you up later Noreen. We have to join the other children in the classroom, so please stop crying and catch hold of Michael's hand and mine and we'll see if we can find your desk in the classroom."

The teacher rang a bell that she pulled out of her coat pocket and asked all the children to follow her into the school. She told us her name was Mrs. Andrews as she led us into the school and through a short corridor to our classroom. There were three rows of wooden desks in the room and she sat Noreen at a desk in the middle row, and I sat at a desk in a row beside her. Noreen had stopped crying and her mind was distracted by the new surroundings, and the chatter and commotion from all the children filing in and finding a desk to sit at. As her day progressed, she seemed to forget about her worries and concerns about not wanting to go to school and played with me and the other children in the playground at lunch break. When school finished at 3:30 p.m., the black Rover was parked in front of the playground, with Aunt Dorothy standing beside it waiting for Noreen and me.

"How was your first day at school?" she enquired as we ran up to the car.

"My teacher's name is Mrs. Andrews," Noreen said. "She has a white rabbit at home and feeds him lettuce. Can we get a rabbit Mummy?"

"We'll see, perhaps one day if you're good."

We stopped off at the post office in the village so that Dorothy could buy a stamp and post a letter. The little post office was also a grocery store that only sold dry goods with a very limited selection. Noreen and I stood looking at all the sweet jars on the shelf behind the counter as Dorothy paid for the stamp and stuck it to the letter in her hand.

"You can pop it in the mailbox slot behind you," the postmistress Mrs. Clark said. "It will be collected first thing in the morning when the postal van brings the mail from Honiton."

"Can we have some sweets?" I asked.

"I'm sorry, I don't have our ration book with me," Dorothy replied. "You'll have to wait until Saturday when we do the grocery shopping."

Because of the war many foods, which included sweets, meat, tea, jam, biscuits, breakfast cereals, cheese, eggs, lard, milk and canned and dried fruit, were rationed. Clothing and petrol were also rationed.

Mrs. Clark reached for the jar of sherbet lemons and removed the black screw-top lid.

"Here you are children," she said, as she offered us each a sweet.

"Thank you," Noreen replied as she reached into the jar and took out a sweet.

I reached into the jar and took out a sweet, but forgot to say thank you.

"What do you say, Michael?" Dorothy asked.

"Thank you Mrs. Clark," I replied.

"That's better. You mustn't forget your manners."

The drive back to Snodwell only took half an hour. When we drove into the farmyard a large green army lorry was parked near the barn with its engine running. Two Italian prisoners of war both wearing distinctive brown uniforms with round yellow patches — one on the back and one on the leg — came out of the hay barn. They climbed into the lorry for the trip back to their POW camp at Goathurst, near the town of Bridgewater (camp number 44), a distance of about 24 miles. They smiled and gave us a wave as we got out of the car. Prisoners were asked if they were willing to work on a farm. Those who agreed to work were labelled

'Cooperators' but were considered traitors by the other prisoners. The prisoners were given a ration of one packet of cigarettes a week and paid approximately five pence a day if they stayed in camp. Those who chose to work outside could earn more. At Snodwell they helped with feeding the cows, milking, cleaning the milking stalls, haymaking and many other farm duties.

The following day, as we turned into the farmyard from school, Dorothy told us that the prisoners wanted to see us before we had tea. They had something to give us. We were excited at the news and wondered what it could be. We climbed the steps into the hay barn to find the two prisoners sitting on a pile of hay with a smile on their faces.

"For you," they said, beckoning us over.

In their hands they each had two wooden sticks with a wooden monkey on a string suspended between the sticks at one end. As they squeezed the sticks together the monkey did acrobatic tricks on the string. They gave us one each and showed us how to make the monkey do his tricks. We thanked them for the toy which they had made, but as they knew very little English we were unable to talk to them.

The two prisoners were only with us for a few more weeks and then we did not see them again. They always had a smile and a wave for Noreen and me whenever they saw us, and although we did not know them, we felt sad when they were gone and we wouldn't see them again. Possibly, now that the war was over, they would be repatriated to their home and families in Italy. At least they did not get shot during the war, and still had their lives ahead of them, which was not the case for many of the troops who so bravely fought for their country. After the war, the British authorities decided that those prisoners who would like to stay in England could be released rather than being shipped back to Italy.

Mark Carlile

A large Guernsey bull named Goldie was kept in one of the buildings attached to the house. He had a pen outside the building where he could get some exercise when he wanted. A ring adorned his nose to facilitate leading him around. My father or Aunt Dorothy would lead him out to a pasture, by using a long pole with a hook on the end which clipped onto his nose ring. He was friendly and never gave any trouble, but like most bulls you could never trust him. He had big curly horns, and was a formidable sight to look at, especially for Noreen and me. I remember my aunt leading him out of the pen one day as Noreen and I stood watching.

"Keep back Noreen," I said. "He likes to eat little girls and has big teeth to chew you up."

"Mum, Michael said the bull will eat me," she called out to her mother.

"Don't listen to him, Noreen," her mother replied. "Goldie is not going to eat anyone. He is just being silly."

While we were living at Snodwell, my Aunt Nancy married a postman, Leonard Pym, who lived in the village of Stockland. Noreen and I were pageboy and girl at their wedding. I was dressed in a sailor suit of blue and white for the occasion.

When my father decided to emigrate to New Zealand in 1947, the farm had to be sold. Following the sale, an auction was held on May 28, 1947 by T. D. Hussey and Son to sell the cattle, implements and the black Rover.

Twenty-five head of Guernsey and cross-bred cattle, a Fordson tractor, numerous implements, and the Rover were all sold. My Aunt Dorothy bought the car for a very reasonable price as there were not many people bidding for it. Most of the people at the auction were farmers who were mainly interested in the farm equipment and livestock.

Snodwell Farm was our home for only a few years but it has fond memories for both Noreen and me.

Eventually Aunt Dorothy and Noreen moved to a small rental flat in the village of Stockland. My Grandmother and I moved to a terraced house at

Evacuation

Richmond Road in the town of Taunton, about 15 miles from Stockland, where my grandfather was living.

Mark Carlile

Chapter 2

Post Farm

In 1948 Dorothy bought Post Farm, located on Post Lane about half a mile from Snodwell Farm. Some of the Post Farm fields adjoin those of Snodwell Farm.

The farm was too much for Dorothy to manage on her own, and as a result, my grandmother and I moved in with her a short time later.

My grandmother did the cooking and looked after the house as well as Noreen and me, which allowed Dorothy to do all the planting and harvesting of crops, and to look after the farm cattle. The only income from the farm was from the sale of milk from the eight cows that Dorothy milked every morning and evening by hand. It was a full-time job for her, and required long hours of work from sun up to sunset, with hardly any free time or days off. It was also very hard physical work with very little assistance, except for harvesting when neighbours and friends gave a hand.

The farmhouse was constructed of stone as were some of the outbuildings. There was no electricity to the property or running water, and no sewer system. The only toilet was an old wooden outhouse at the bottom of the garden about twenty yards from the house. Water was hand pumped from a well in the yard, and carried into the house in a bucket, and stored in a large water tub.

Mark Carlile

The house had four rooms on the ground level which consisted of a dining room, sitting room, a long narrow kitchen which Gran called a scullery, and a small bathroom. In the scullery, Gran did the washing and ironing, cleaned the milk churns, made clotted cream by scalding the milk from the dairy, did the cooking, and cleaned the dishes and utensils. Water was heated in a built-in wood-fired cast-iron copper. Water had to be added and removed with a bucket. Logs were added through an opening in the stonework, and an opening below provided a flow of air and a place to remove the fallen ashes. The stove was also wood fired as were many stoves in the old farm houses. The dining room and living room had wood-burning fireplaces, which were the only source of heat. An oil lamp hung from the ceiling over the large wooden table, and the only radio we had, powered by two large batteries, sat in the window seat. On the upper level there were three bedrooms.

The bathroom in the house was very small, it consisted of a countertop with a small sink that drained into a bucket. A wooden stairway at the side of the bathroom led to the upper level bedrooms.

Gran would give us both a bath once a week in a steel bathtub, placed in front of the fire in the living room. Noreen and I bathed in the same water. Gran had to heat the water in the copper and carry it in a bucket to the bathtub.

"I want to go first," I said.

"Noreen is a girl so you have to let her go first," Gran insisted. "You can go first next time."

"Oh, okay," I reluctantly said.

The water would become a little cooler after Noreen had bathed and dressed while I waited in the dining room. Gran would warm it a little by adding another bucket of hot water before I bathed. The only benefit about going second was that the steel tub was more full. We spent most evenings in the dining room as there was always a fire there in the winter time, and it was the warmest room in the house. Gran often spent her evenings knitting socks and pullovers for Noreen and me because clothing was expensive, and clothing rationing did not end until March of 1949.

Noreen and I attended Summerlands School, a private school in New Street in Honiton, a small town about six miles from Post Farm. There were no buses to this school, which resulted in Dorothy having to drive us to school in the car and pick us up in the afternoon when school came out. Nearly every morning our Collie dog, Tinker, would sit in the road and bark to see us off to school.

Tinker was black with a white underbelly and legs and had a small brown flash over his eyes. He was sometimes vocal but would never bite or act aggressively. He was a very friendly dog and always joined Dorothy when she went to find the cows and bring them in for milking. I don't know where he came from, he just seemed to be there. Perhaps we inherited him with the farm.

We only attended Summerlands School for a little while, after which we went to Honiton Primary School, a public school. A school bus stopped at the top of Post Lane to pick us up and take us to school. Petrol was still on ration at the time, so Dorothy was pleased that she would no longer have to drive us to school. Petrol rationing did not end until the twenty-sixth of May 1950. We generally walked the half mile from the farm to the top of the lane where it intersected with the old Roman road. If it was raining, Dorothy would drive us to the top of the lane in the car. On the corner of the old Roman road and Post Lane, there was a wooden platform about four feet high built into the hedge where Dorothy put the milk churns for the milk truck to collect. The truck would pick up the full churns and leave empty churns in their place. When it was raining, which was quite often in the winter, Noreen and I would shelter from the rain underneath the milk churn platform until the bus came to take us to school.

A few months later the school bus changed its route, and no longer stopped at the top of Post Lane. As a result, we had to walk about a mile along the old Roman road to the crossroad at the Rising Sun Farm, where the bus would stop to pick us up at eight-thirty in the morning. Dorothy often drove us in the car, especially if we were late leaving the farm or if the weather was bad. It was a much longer walk for us, but we soon got used to the long walk in the mornings and afternoons when the bus dropped us off at four o'clock. One of my school chums, Derek Boilen, lived on a farm halfway between Post Lane and the bus stop, and walked home with us along the Roman road. The Boilen's farm was down a long muddy lane on the same side of the Roman road as Post Lane. One day after school we walked home with Derek and met his mother and father.

"Would you like some biscuits and orange juice?" his mother asked. "I have just taken the biscuits out of the oven."

"Yes please," we both answered in unison.

We sat by a big log fire in the kitchen enjoying the snack and juice and talking to Mrs. Boilen before leaving to walk home.

"Where do you live?" Mr. Boilen asked.

"Post Farm," Noreen replied. "Do you know where that is?"

"Yes, I do. It is just at the bottom of the common at the end of our lane. It may be quicker for you to go through the five-bar gate at the end of our lane, and across the common which would bring you out by Mr. Manley's house. It will be quite a bit shorter than following the roadway. Derek will show you when you are ready to leave."

"Thank you. We'll try it," I replied.

After we left, Derek walked with us to the end of the lane and pointed the way to a cow track and the direction to Mr. Manley's house. We climbed up and over the five-bar gate and took the sloping track across the common. The track was overgrown with ferns, and disappeared in places, but we followed it downhill until we could see the roof of Mr. Manley's cottage. As we approached the cottage, Noreen asked, "Do you think he will be angry with us for trespassing through his property?"

"He might if he sees us. We have to run fast when we get to his yard. When I say run, run as fast as you can and get over the gate and run home."

"Okay," Noreen replied.

As we got near the yard, there appeared to be no sign of Mr. Manley. Smoke was billowing from the cottage chimney, and a few chickens scratched around in the yard. We crouched down in the ferns as we got nearer in case he came out, but he was nowhere in sight. Our shoes, legs and socks were wet now because water from a recent shower had made the ferns and long scrub grass wet. We crouched for a few more minutes and then I said "Run".

Noreen was ahead of me but I was right behind her. The chickens in the yard scattered and started clucking as we raced through the yard, climbed the five-bar gate at the entrance, and raced down Post Lane to the safety of our farm.

When we went in the front door and removed our shoes and socks, Gran wanted to know why we were wet. We told her the story about visiting the Boilens on the way home, explaining that it was a much shorter and quicker route home across the common. She did not seem to object.

"I don't know what old Mr. Manley will say if he catches you trespassing on his property. You two better be careful if you do it again."

She handed us a towel and a clean pair of socks to put on as we sat by the fire drying our legs and cold feet.

"What's for supper?" I asked.

Mark Carlile

"Rabbit stew," Gran replied.
"Not that again," I said. "We had that last night."
"Well, we're having it again," Gran replied.

We had a large garden at the front of the house, half of which was flowerbeds. The other half was a vegetable garden and chicken coop and run, and some waste ground. At the bottom of the garden next to the outhouse, a wooden gate led to a large apple orchard. At the bottom of the orchard a five-bar wooden gate opened into a ten-acre field with a wooded area beyond it.

The farmyard at the side of the house had a field-stone surface. A hay barn was adjoined to one side of the house. Milking stalls opened onto the farmyard as well as two open-fronted cow sheds, for shelter in bad weather. Most days the cows were turned out into the fields. At the end of the sheds a five-bar wooden gate opened into the apple orchard. Behind the cowsheds and milking stalls a 15-acre field sloped steeply up to a wooded area of oak, ash, field maple and hazel trees. At the opposite end of the house was Post Lane. The lane had only a narrow grass verge between the house and the tarmac surface and ran steeply uphill.

Mr. Manley's cottage was about fifty yards up the hill on the opposite side of the road. It was an old stone cottage with a thatched roof. He had a brightly painted horse-drawn Romany caravan in the yard by the hedge. There was a five-bar wooden entry gate to his yard. We were told that he was once a Gypsy, or didicoy, as my Uncle Len, a village postman in Stockland, was fond of calling them.

"They are thieves and rogues." He would often say. "You can't trust them. They'll steal anything."

Typically, the gypsies would roam the countryside looking for any casual or seasonal work they could find, and would generally park their caravans on a piece of rough ground or a common at the edge of towns and villages. In the summer months, they sometimes moved from farm to farm to help with the harvesting of crops, picking cherries, strawberries, and blackcurrants, as well as beans and peas and other vegetables. They often made a little money by going door to door selling wooden handmade clothes pegs and basket in the winter time. The men would also sharpen knives. Some people did not trust them and considered them to be thieves. Many a time they would be moved on from their campsite by the police or an angry farmer who did not want them on his land.

Mr. Manley had retired from the wandering life and settled down in a conventional home. Noreen and I did not meet him for quite a while. He was a white-haired old man with a beard. We occasionally saw him in the yard in front of his house, sometimes chopping firewood. He would wave to us as we walked up the lane to catch the school bus, and we would wave back and hurry past. We had no reason to fear or distrust him because he was once a Gypsy, but because of their bad reputation and dislike by Uncle Len, we tended to try to avoid him.

Our neighbour Mrs. Bond, who had three children, lived in a cottage about a hundred yards down the lane from Post Farm on the same side of the lane. The oldest boy, Peter, was thirteen, his sister, Linda, was nine and younger brother, Kenny, was four. Mrs. Bond raised and sold chickens as well as their eggs. Their garden adjoined the bottom of our garden, separated by a small creek. Peter and Linda sometimes walked up the lane with us in the morning to catch the school bus if we happened to leave at the same time.

Land at the driveway entrance to Snodwell Farm belonged to Post Farm. Dorothy planted a five-acre field with kale for the cows on one side of the driveway. On the other side a large common covered with bracken, tall ferns, scrub grass and yellow flowering prickly gorse extended up a steep hillside to a large fifty-acre field. Dorothy planted the field with grass for hay for use as animal fodder. In an adjacent thirty-acre field she planted corn. Dorothy sometimes used the common for grazing the cows. She had a large Nissen hut (a semicircular structure of corrugated steel) by the entrance to the field where she stored the corn. One day, the door was left slightly ajar. A Guernsey cow managed to get into the hut and gorged itself on corn. When Dorothy discovered the animal, it was lying on its side severely bloated with gas from the fermented corn in its stomach. The vet would be needed if this cow was to be saved. She ran home and got the car and drove along the old Roman road to the intersection of the A30 to Jauncey's Garage, where she often bought petrol and had her car serviced.

Mr. Jauncey had a phone he said Dorothy could use any time she needed to make a call. After making the call to the vet, she left two pence on the counter to cover the cost of the call. Fortunately, the vet was home, and he said he would come straight away. When the vet finally arrived, he poked a hole in the cow's stomach and released the gas. If Dorothy hadn't discovered the cow when she did, the vet said it would have died.

Christmas was a special time of the year for Noreen and me because we still believed in Father Christmas. We would leave a pillowcase by the fireplace in the living room along with a note to Father Christmas.

Every year, Gran and Dorothy would take us to the pantomime at a theatre in Exeter. Pantomimes were developed in England and were generally performed between Christmas and the New Year. They are a musical comedy stage production designed for family entertainment. We saw Jack and the Bean Stalk, Robin Hood and His Merry Men, Sleeping Beauty, and Snow White and the Seven Dwarfs, and probably a few more. We always looked forward to the pantomime and would act out some of the parts in the weeks following our visit. Noreen made a good Maid Marian with her long hair. I would play Robin Hood and made a bow and arrows from branches we cut from trees in the hedgerow. In the woods at the top of the hill at the back of the cow sheds, we made a camp from branches and tree foliage that we cut down, and from dried branches we found on the ground. We would play for hours in our imaginary world of Sherwood Forest, outfoxing the Sheriff of Nottingham and his men as they chased us through the forest. Our dog Tinker, who followed us everywhere, would often join in. The wooded area extended for a long way and was very thick in places, so we had to be careful we didn't get disoriented and lost. We rarely told Gran or Dorothy where we were going, so if we did get lost it could take a long time before we were found. Fortunately, that never happened.

Boxing Day in England was a national holiday and is generally spent with friends and family eating the leftovers from Christmas Day. There are many theories as to how it originated, but many think it was a day off for the servants when they received a 'Christmas Box' from the employer of the house. It is also a day renown for fox hunting and other hunting sports. Unless you were rich or knew someone who had an estate and bred deer, deer hunting was out of the question.

On Boxing Day, Uncle Len and some of his village friends in Stockland came up to Post Farm to hunt rabbits. Dorothy, Noreen and I would walk up to the top of Post Lane where they often hunted, and stand on the top of the hedge watching. Tinker was kept at home by Gran because we did not want to risk him being shot by accident as he was fond of chasing rabbits. Len had a ferret that he put in the rabbit hole in the hedge to chase the rabbit out. Len and his friends stood by with shotguns to shoot the rabbit when it bolted from the hole. Sometimes, they got lucky when the rabbit holes were interconnected, because two or three rabbits would bolt out running across the field. Some got away before being shot if the shooters were not quick enough or their aim was off. Occasionally the ferret got lost in the hole or refuse to come out, and they had to dig it out of the hedge with spades. Len gutted and clean all the rabbits and always gave Dorothy some to take home. The remnants from cleaning general provide an evening feast for the local foxes.

Chapter 3

Life on the Farm

It was a carefree life for Noreen and me because we had the fields, woods and common land to explore and wander around, when we were home from school on weekends and in the evenings.

The people who lived at Snodwell Farm had a little five-year-old boy named David. His parents did not want him walking to the top of Post Lane on his own, so his mother would walk with him to the end of the driveway to the farm and wait for Noreen and me to come by. He would then walk with us to the top of Post Lane to catch the bus to school. Peter and Linda Bond, our neighbour's children, would oftentimes be with us for our morning walk, to catch the bus.

After the school bus stopped picking us up at the top of Post Lane, we had the much longer walk to the crossroads at Rising Sun Farm. We had to leave home about thirty minutes earlier because of the extra mile we had to walk along the old Roman road. Although we played and had fun during the walk, I don't think we missed the bus very often. We very rarely saw a vehicle at that time of the morning. Occasionally we'd see a farm tractor pulling an implement or a load of hay as we walked down the middle of the long straight road.

There were a number of farm children of various ages who caught the bus at the Rising Sun. One morning after a heavy overnight rainstorm, there was a large puddle of water just inside one of the fields at the crossroads. The gate to the field had been conveniently left open. Whilst we waited for the bus, several of us boys were entertaining ourselves by throwing stones, we found in a pile by the hedge, into the muddy puddle to see who could make the biggest splash. Suddenly, Peter Bond and another older boy grabbed hold of me, one by the arms and one by the legs and lifted me off the ground.

"Put me down Peter," I yelled. "The bus is coming."

"No, it's not," he replied. "You're going in the water."

"No no, please don't do that." I screamed.

They swung me back and forth over the water which terrified me. I thought they were going to throw me into the middle of the puddle. I was yelling and screaming for them to stop, and struggling to get free as best I could, but they took no notice. They stopped swinging me and gradually lowered me into the cold muddy water until my backside was wet. Then they released me. The short grey trousers and underpants I was wearing were both sodden with water. Water ran down my legs leaving muddy streaks on my bare legs and made the tops of my long wool socks wet and discolored. I thought about going home immediately.

Just then, the bus arrived. I was feeling discomfort as I made my way to a window seat near the back behind most of the other children. I stared out the window feeling very upset and very uncomfortable. Peter Bond came up the aisle and sat beside me. The seat of the bus was now wet from muddy water that had soaked into my trousers. I was feeling very cold. Peter could see that I was extremely annoyed at him as I stared out the window and refused to look at or talk to him. He quietly whispered in my ear.

"You won't tell your Gran will you, because I will be in trouble if you do?"

I refused to reply or look at him. By the time we arrived at our school in Honiton, my pants were starting to dry out a little from the heat of my body and the absorption from the bus seat. When I got off the bus I wondered if the other kids would see the wet patch on the seat of my trousers and think that I had peed my pants, or worse with the brown mud streaks down my legs.

We made our way to our classroom and took our seats at the wood and steel framed desks. At the first opportunity I got, I put up my hand to go to the toilet. In the toilet I used wet toilet paper to wipe off the brown streaks from my legs, and I stuffed some toilet paper inside my underpants to soak up some of the dampness. By mid-day when we went for lunch my trousers were almost dry. I told Noreen what Peter Bond had done to me.

"Are you going to tell Gran?" Noreen asked.

"I don't think I will," I replied. "If I do, Peter will be in trouble with his mother."

When we arrived home that evening Gran wanted to know how I had gotten so dirty. "I fell in a puddle at school," I told her. "One of my class friends pushed me and I slipped."

"You better take off your trousers and socks and I will get you some clean clothes to put on," she said. "I'll have to wash your dirty clothes."

I didn't think that my clothes were very dirty, but Gran always wanted me to look clean and smart when I went to school. For a few weeks I hated Peter and would have nothing to do with him. I tried to avoid walking with Peter and Linda on the way to catch the bus in the morning, and if we did see them during our morning walk, I wouldn't speak to him.

Gran and Dorothy had very little money, but they always did their best to save wherever possible and provide Noreen and me with a birthday gift. They would also fill the pillowcases that we hung up for Father Christmas.

One day when Dorothy and Gran drove into Honiton to do some banking and shopping, they picked

Noreen and me up from school. Noreen needed a new pair of shoes, which Dorothy shopped for first. While they were shopping, Gran, and I visited the toy shop next door to the shoe shop. I didn't realize it at the time but Gran was trying to get some idea of what Father Christmas should bring me. There was a red four-wheeled handcart on the floor with the scooters and bicycles. The sales assistant explained that it could be ridden and guided by a swivelling handle that was attached to the articulating front wheels.

"What do you think of that?" Gran asked.

"It's nice," I replied, not really thinking too much about it. I was more interested in the cowboy outfits and toy cars.

After we browsed throughout the store, Gran said it was time to go.

"Just a bit longer," I said.

"No, we have to go. Noreen and Dorothy will be waiting, and we still have to go to the bank."

When we left the toy store, Noreen and Dorothy were just coming out of the shoe shop. Noreen was wearing a brand new pair of tan leather shoes with two crossover straps with gold buckles. She was carrying a cardboard box that contained her old shoes.

"Look at my new shoes," she said to Gran and me. "Don't they look smart?"

"Yes they are nice," Gran replied. "You'll have to take care of them."

After Dorothy had done her banking, we drove back to Post Farm. Noreen and I were in the back seat of Dorothy's black Rover and Gran was in the front with Dorothy. Every now and again I noticed Noreen looking at her new shoes. She seemed to be very proud of them. New clothing was a special treat for us because we could not afford a lot of new clothes, and clothing was still on ration at the time.

I frequently got a sick feeling riding in the back seat of the car, depending on how twisty the roads were. Dorothy often had to stop for me to get out and sit on the running board with my head in my hands while I got some fresh air and waited for my stomach to settle. Occasionally I would be sick. Sometimes I only had to set foot in the car and I would get a sick feeling just from the smell of the interior. It was really strange.

Linda Bond told us one day when we were walking to school that there was no Father Christmas — it's your parents. We often wondered how a little fat man could climb down the chimney, and how he could visit all the children in one night. It did not come as a shock to Noreen and me but we were sad that the myth had been destroyed. We continued to hang up our pillowcases on Christmas Eve to be filled by Father Christmas, and always went to bed when we were told, to be sure Gran and Dorothy had lots of time to fill our pillowcases. It was still a magical time that we loved so much and always looked forward to for several more years, even after Linda had spilled the beans.

One Christmas will always stick in my mind. We had spent the evening putting the final decorations on the Christmas tree in the sitting room. Dorothy had cut the tree down from the woods at the top of the hill behind the cow sheds.

Gran had a big log fire burning in the stone fireplace which she only lit on special occasions, and on bath night in the winter time. We were generally allowed to stay up a little later on Christmas Eve because we were on holiday from school. When it was time to go to bed, we put our pillowcases by the fireplace and Gran got some hot water in a kettle and we helped her fill our rubber hot water bottles. Noreen had a pink one and mine was blue. We held the bottles by the neck as Gran carefully poured in the water and screwed in the stoppers. Then she hung the bottles upside down to make sure the stoppers did not leak. We climbed the squeaky wooden staircase to our bedrooms clutching the hot rubber bottle to our chest, feeling the welcome warmth quickly penetrating

Mark Carlile

There was no heat in the bedrooms and the bed felt very cold as I placed the hot water bottle in the bed about where my feet would rest. I quickly undressed leaving my clothes in a heap at the foot of the bed, put on my cold flannel pajamas which were on the pillow and climbed into bed. It was good to feel the warmth of the hot water bottle, which was already starting to cool down to the point where I could keep it between my feet. I could hear the rain tapping on the window behind my bed as I lay in bed and wondered what I would get for Christmas. The wind was starting to pick up. I could hear it rustling the leaves on the trees across the lane. The rain got heavier and began pounding on the window as the wind gusts got stronger. It was a comforting sound as I lay there thinking about Christmas morning and slowly drifted off to sleep.

On Christmas morning Noreen crept out of the bedroom that she shared with her mother and tiptoed to my bedside.

"Let's go downstairs and see if Father Christmas has been," she whispered, trying not to wake Gran in her bed on the far side of the large room I shared with her.

We slowly made our way down the squeaky stairs trying to be as quiet as possible, without waking Gran and Dorothy and dashed into the living room to see if Father Christmas had paid us a visit.

Our pillowcases were beside the fireplace which still had warm embers from the night before. They were about half full with presents, and several presents were below the Christmas tree, which included the little red wagon that Gran and I had looked at in the toy shop in Honiton. I wondered why she had bought that as I could not think what I could do with it. I was really disappointed when I saw it. I would have much preferred a cowboy outfit, I thought. Noreen had a large box under the tree wrapped up in red paper imprinted with holly. She quickly tore away the paper to find a doll with curly blond hair and a pink dress and brown shoes. She loved dolls, and played with them for hours, pushing them around in the pram she had gotten for her birthday.

We started going through the presents in our pillowcases. Games, books, bags of sweets, small toys, pencil and pens, painting sets, stencils, comics and many other small gifts that we received from Father Christmas. After a while we had all the gifts spread out on the floor and were sampling some of the licorice-all-sorts that we both had. Gran was soon up and came downstairs to see what the excitement was about. Dorothy soon followed, and after a quick cup of tea, went out to do the milking.

Gran sat on the couch and watched us looking and playing with some of the gifts.

"Do you like your wagon Michael?" she asked me.

"It's alright," I replied. "I don't know what I will do with it. It is only good for putting things in to move to another place," I told her.

Her face dropped and tears came to her eyes.

"I thought you said you liked it when we were in the toy shop," she replied.

"It's not much use to me, I can't think when I would use it. I don't want it."

Gran left the room. She was obviously upset that she had disappointed me.

"Breakfast is ready," Gran shouted from the dining room about twenty minutes later. "Come and sit up."

We sat at the dining room table in our pajamas eating our cereal, Noreen looking at one of her new books, and I was looking at a cowboy comic.

Gran came in from the scullery with her toast on a plate and a cup of tea and sat down to have her breakfast.

"You can ride that wagon," she said. "Just take it up to the top of the hill by Mr. Manley's place and ride it down the hill. It has stopped raining now, so you will be able to try it after breakfast."

Mark Carlile

Gran made us a fried egg on fried bread and made sure we drank our orange juice before leaving the table.

After we had looked at and played with some of our gifts from Father Christmas, we took the little red wagon into the lane and pulled it up the hill to Mr. Manley's house.

"I'll get in," I said to Noreen, "and you can give me a push."

It didn't need much of a push before the little red wagon was rolling downhill at quite a speed. The first thing that came to my mind was how do I stop it? I let it roll as it went faster and faster down the hill, past the farmhouse and came to a stop. I got out quickly and grabbed the handle and pulled it back up the hill again.

"Your turn Noreen," I said. "Get in."

"I'm not going in it," she replied. "It goes too fast."

"I'll come with you."

"Alright, if you sit in front and steer," she said.

I sat up front with one leg bent up, the other over the edge of the cart resting on the ground to prevent the cart from running down the hill, while Noreen got in. Noreen climbed in behind me with her hands on my shoulders and when she was ready, I brought my foot in and we started to roll. We rolled faster and faster down the hill to just past the farmhouse and came to a gentle stop. Our dog, Tinker, thought it was great fun. He ran down the hill beside us barking all the way down the hill.

On the next run I persuaded Noreen to ride on her own. She was a little apprehensive at first, but agreed to try it after I told her to drive the cart into the grass verge if she wanted to stop. We had a lot of fun with the cart and had been riding it for well over an hour when Gran came out to see what all the noise was about. She watched us riding down the hill with Tinker barking and following behind. She was so pleased that we liked her Christmas present and were having fun with it.

For the rest of the morning we sat on the floor in the living room by the roaring log fire and played with the other gifts from our pillowcases.

"Don't eat too many of those sweets," Gran said when she came into the room. "Dinner will be ready soon."

I didn't see Peter Bond very much except when we walked to school in the mornings. I had forgiven him for dipping my bum in the water and was talking to him again. One Saturday morning he came walking down the lane and stopped to chat when he saw me riding the little red cart down the hill.

"If you'd like to walk down to the bridge with me I have something to show you," he said.

Down the lane from our farm just past the Bond's house, Post Lane ran through a little stream. Most of the year it was just shallow water that ran across the road. A car was able to drive through except for sometimes in the winter after heavy rain. When it flooded, it became impassable to most vehicles except for farm tractors. Noreen and I nearly always wore rubber boots around the farm, especially in the winter. Wellingtons they were called, or Wellies we called them. The name originated from a boot developed by the Duke of Wellington in the 18th century. Sometimes we went down to this little stream wearing our Wellies and played around in the water.

Just before the stream was a small, grassy field that was usually covered in daffodils in the springtime. The field belonged to Mrs. Bond. When the daffodils flowered, Noreen and I picked a bunch of daffodils for our kitchen because they looked beautiful and smelled so nice. We often pick mushrooms in this field as well which Gran would fry for breakfast. Mrs. Bond said that the reason for mushrooms being in this field was because it was once a pasture for horses.

A little footbridge for pedestrians crossed the stream. Peter and I sat on it when we arrived at the

Mark Carlile

stream with our legs dangling over the stream. Peter took a small square tin out of his pocket and said "I have just started smoking. Would you like to try it?"

"All right," I replied. "How do you do it?"

Peter had a little cardboard pouch of cigarette papers and pulled a paper out of it. He then put some tobacco from a tin onto the cigarette paper and carefully spread it out all along the paper. Then he rolled it up between his fingers, licked the edge of the paper and rolled it a little more until the paper stuck. It looked like a white tube with a little tobacco protruding from the ends. He tore off one end and put it in his mouth and lit it with a match from a box of matches from his pocket.

"Do you want to try it?" he asked, handing me the cigarette.

I took it and sucked on it once and began to choke from the smoke in my mouth. Peter quickly took it back as I continued to cough and choke. He puffed on it again and said, "You sucked too hard, just do it gently."

After I recovered from my choking, I tried it again, but this time took a gentle puff. We passed the cigarette back and forth between us, until it was burnt very short, and Peter tossed it into the stream.

"I feel a little sick and dizzy," I said.

"That will go away in a minute. You took too big a puff to begin with. You just have to take small puffs until you are used to the smoke in your mouth — don't tell anyone about this, or I will be in real trouble with my mother and your Gran."

"I won't say anything," I replied.

I went down to the footbridge several times after that to smoke a cigarette with Peter. I soon got used to it and did not choke anymore, but it still made me a little dizzy sometimes.

When Peter was old enough, he bought a motorbike. It had a fish tail exhaust and a gear change on the tank. I think he said it was a BSA. At nighttime when he returned home, we would often hear the sound of his motorbike way up the lane. The sound got louder and louder as he approached. It made lots of noise as he came past the farm house, often waking Dorothy and Gran from their sleep.

One day Peter came up the lane on his motorbike and stopped when he saw me in the lane with my red cart.

"Would you like a ride on my motorbike?" he asked, as he turned the engine off. "It's really fast."

Gran was in the garden and came out to the lane when she heard him stop to talk to me.

"Can I go for a ride on Peter's motorbike?" I asked her.

"I don't think you should," she said. "Peter is a new driver so I don't think you should go."

"Please Gran, I really want to go, please, please."

"Alright," she said, "but don't go too fast Peter, I don't want him falling off and hurting himself."

I climbed on the back of Peter's motorbike and caught hold of his coat with both hands. Peter pulled the goggles he had pushed up on his forehead back down over his eyes. Then kick-started the motorbike and revved the throttle a little.

"Are you ready?" he asked.

"Yes, I'm ready."

"Hold on tight," Gran shouted over the noise of the engine.

Peter revved it again, pulled a lever on the side of the petrol tank and with a jerk we set off up Post Lane. It was the first time I had ever been on a motorbike. I hung on as tightly as I could, especially as we went around the bends in the lane. Peter sounded his horn before each bend because if he met a car he would have to pull to the side and stop. The lane was so narrow that he would not be able to pass a car.

When we got to the entrance of Snodwell Lane just before the steep hill, Peter stopped. He turned to me and said "Lean forward as we go up the hill."

Mark Carlile

We started to climb the steep hill very rapidly, the engine roaring loudly as Peter accelerated until we reached the crest of the hill. The lane levelled off to a straight flat section eventually coming to the junction with the old Roman road. He turned right at the junction and shouted back to me to hang on. He accelerated quickly, and the engine ran faster and faster and made lots of noise. I watched the telephone poles racing past and the blast of air swept back my hair and flapped my coat and trousers as if it were trying to tear everything off me. I had never experienced anything like this before. We soon got to the Royal Oak crossroad where a left turn would take us to Stockland. Peter stopped and turned around to go back.

"How fast did we go?" I shouted to him.

"Seventy," he replied. "I will try to go faster as we go back."

He accelerated again as I clung on for dear life, the blast of air trying to pull me off, as it tugged at everything with a little more force this time. When we slowed down to turn into Post Lane, Peter stopped again. I asked how fast we went this time.

"Almost eighty," he replied. "Did you enjoy it?"

"Yes I did, it was fun."

We slowly drove back to Post Farm, my first motorbike ride coming to an end. He dropped me off and accelerated down the lane and back to his home. I never had another ride on Peter's motorbike, but the memory of that first ride was something I always remember. I related the experience to my classmates at school and friends and relatives who visited the farm.

Chapter 4

Guy Fawkes Day

The exact date of birth of Guy Fawkes in Stonegate, in the city of York, is unknown. Because he was baptised in the church of St. Michael le Belfrey in York on April 16, 1570, and the usual time between birth and baptism being three days, he was most likely born on April 13th.

In 1579 when Fawkes was only eight years old, his father died. His mother remarried to a Catholic a few years later. In 1591 Fawkes sold the estate that he inherited from his father and travelled to Spain to fight in the Eighty Years War for Catholic Spain. He later became a junior officer and was recommended for captaincy. He sought support in Spain for the Catholic rebellion in England. In 1604 Guy Fawkes became involved with a small group of English Catholics who plotted to assassinate the Protestant King James. The first meeting of the five conspirators was held at the Duck and Drake Inn in the Strand district of London, on May 20, 1604. One of the conspirators, Robert Catesby, had proposed at an earlier meeting with Thomas Wintour and John Wright to kill the King and government by blowing up the Houses of Parliament at the Palace of Westminster with gunpowder.

The plotters purchased the lease to an undercroft (cellar or storage room) that was directly below the

Mark Carlile

House of Lords. It was the perfect hiding place for the 36 barrels of gunpowder they brought in, in July of 1605. The threat of plague had delayed the opening of parliament until the fifth of November. Following a series of meetings, it was decided that Guy Fawkes would light the fuse and make his escape across the River Thames.

Some of the conspirators were concerned for the safety of fellow Catholics who would be present in the Houses of Parliament on the 5th of November, and sent an anonymous letter of warning to Lord Monteagle, warning him to stay away. The letter was shown to King James. King James ordered a search of the cellars below Parliament and Guy Fawkes was discovered leaving the cellar in the early morning hours and was arrested. The gunpowder was found hidden under a pile of firewood. Guy Fawkes admitted, after his interrogation, his intention to blow up the House of Lords, and expressed regret he failure to do so. King James ordered his transfer to the Tower of London, and his torture in an effort to find the names of his co-conspirators. After severe torture, he eventually gave up the names of the other people involved.

The trial of Guy Fawkes and seven of his co-conspirators took place on the 27th of January 1606, and all were found guilty of high treason. Their fate was to be hanged, drawn and quartered. Fawkes and three others were dragged from the Tower of London to Old Palace Yard at Westminster, opposite the building they tried to blow up, and the other three were hanged, drawn and quartered. When Guy Fawkes climbed the ladder to the hangman's noose, he was thought to have avoided the agony of hanging by jumping off the ladder with the rope around his neck, thereby breaking his neck. His body was then quartered and his body parts distributed and displayed as a warning to others.

Londoners were encouraged to celebrate the King's escape each 5th of November by lighting bonfires. It would later become a custom in England to celebrate each 5th of November, by lighting bonfires accompanied by fireworks and the burning of an effigy of Guy Fawkes on the fire, to commemorate the failure of the plot.

About three weeks before the 5th of November each year, Noreen and I would start to make preparations for the celebration of the failure of the gunpowder plot. Dorothy said we could have a fire in the lower field as long as we keep it well away from the hedge. The lower field is what Dorothy called the field at the bottom of the orchard. It was well away from the house and the farm buildings, which a stray spark could burn down very easily.

We started collecting anything that would burn for our bonfire. Wood from around the field, fallen branches from our apple trees, any garbage that Gran wanted burnt. If we needed more, we dragged out any dead wood we could find from the nearby woods. Hours were spent dragging out and pulling the wood across the field to our ever-increasing pile of wood and burnable waste.

We always built an effigy of Guy Fawkes, which was easy to construct. A fallen tree branch was used for the vertical member of the cross we constructed, and another branch formed the cross member. Dorothy had a box of used binder twine that she had cut from hay bales in the barn. Some of this strong twine was used to bind the cross member of the cross to the vertical member. Gran was pestered to search for an old pair of trousers and an old shirt or pullover that we could use for the effigy. We stuffed them with dried grass, waste hay and straw found lying about the yard, and old newspaper. Once stuffed, we tied the stuffed trousers and shirt to the cross with binder twine. The guy's head was made from cloth or an old potato sack formed into a ball and stuffed with grass and tied onto the body. An old hat was fastened to the head to complete our guy.

Mark Carlile

The cross with our guy strapped to it was jammed into the top of the pile of wood and waste of our bonfire. Children in towns and cities often put their Guy Fawkes effigy in a wheelbarrow and pushed it around the neighbourhood asking people for a 'penny for the guy'. With the money they collected, they bought fireworks. Because Noreen and I lived on a farm, it was not practical to do that.

Clark's grocery shop in Stockland, which was also the post office, always sold boxes of fireworks in various sizes when Guy Fawkes Day approached. Each Saturday, Dorothy and Gran went to Stockland to shop for tinned and packaged groceries at Mrs. Clark's shop. She did not sell vegetables as it was only a small shop, and we didn't need fresh vegetables as we grew our own. Noreen and I always went along to get sweets. Mrs. Clark had a good selection of sweets in large glass jars which she kept on a shelf behind the counter. Sweets were sold loose and were scooped into a paper bag according to the weight you selected. Noreen and I looked through the boxes of fireworks as Dorothy and Gran did the grocery shopping. We tried to select a box that contained a few rockets, some bangers, jumping jacks and a selection of others. If we chose too expensive a box, Gran would tell us to choose a different box. We always got a box of fireworks and I would generally carry the box out to the car to look at the contents as we drove home.

After spending a lot of time building our bonfire, which we continued to add to right up to the 5th of November, and making the guy, we hoped it didn't rain. If rain made everything wet, it would make lighting our bonfire much more difficult or impossible.

When Guy Fawkes Day arrived, we got prepared early for the event. Old newspapers were gathered for stuffing at the base of the bonfire for lighting it, a bottle for putting the rockets in to direct them skyward, a box of matches to light the bonfire and fireworks, and some torches to light our way through the orchard and across the lower field to our bonfire.

Gran made sure we were dressed warm with a coat, gloves and a scarf because the weather was typically cold in November, with frost forming on the ground overnight. Dorothy milked the cows about 5:30 p.m., and generally finished about 7:30 p.m., then she would come in for a cup of tea and a biscuit. We had to wait for Dorothy because she always lit the bonfire and set off the fireworks.

As Dorothy was drinking her tea, Gran said, "Have you two children been to the bottom of the garden? You should probably go because you don't want to return to go during the fireworks."

Gran always asked this before we went to bed at night. She wanted to make sure we had been to the outhouse before going to bed.

Noreen and I slipped on our Wellington boots, took the torch off the windowsill where it was normally kept, and walk down the path to the outhouse at the bottom of the garden. One of us would go in with the torch whilst the other waited outside in the darkness. It was normally very dark unless the moon was shining, which it rarely did in the winter time. The only thing that could be seen, as your eyes adjusted to the darkness, was the shadowy shapes of trees and bushes, and you could hear the trickle of the stream outside the garden gate in the silence of the night. Inside the outhouse it was pitch black because there were no windows, so you had to have a torch. There were lots of spider webs in there and it was quite creepy because you never knew if a big spider would drop down on you at any minute. We didn't have toilet rolls. Gran would cut up a newspaper into squares, poke a hole in the corner with a pair of scissors and put a loop of binder twine through the hole. The paper could then be hung on a nail on the outhouse wall. We also kept a newspaper on the bench seat of the outhouse, in case we ran out of newspaper squares hanging on the wall.

Mark Carlile

When we returned to the kitchen Dorothy was just finishing her tea and biscuits.

"Are you ready to go and light the bonfire?" she asked.

"Yes, we have everything ready," Noreen replied.

Gran was sitting in the armchair beside the fireplace knitting a pullover she had been working on for several weeks and was almost finished.

"I won't be coming down with you," she said. "It is too cold and I don't want to trip and fall in the dark, so you children enjoy yourself and be careful."

We dressed in our warm clothes, put on our boots and grabbed the box of fireworks, old newspapers, bottle, matches and torches and went out the scullery door.

It was very dark and cold as we crossed the yard. Tinker bounded up and joined us as we opened the gate to the orchard. A dew was starting to form on the grass as we made our way through the orchard. The water droplets flicked up by our boots sparkled in the light of our torches as we made our way to the gate into the lower field and our bonfire.

We stuffed newspaper into the base of the bonfire in several locations, along with small twigs that we broke off from some of the branches for kindling. When we were ready, Dorothy lit the newspapers and our fire was started. Because the wood was dead tree branches that were quite dry it did not take long before we had a blazing fire going. Sparks crackled as they shot high into the air, the orange and red glow from the blazing wood pile illuminated the field and provided us with a welcome heat on this cold, damp evening. Our Guy Fawkes was soon starting to get singed by the flames licking around it, but still stood tall and proud on the woodpile.

Dorothy took out one of our fireworks from the box, sat it in the soft dirt of a mole hill, lit the blue paper and quickly ran away from it. It fizzled, then flared up in a bright red plume of fire that lit up the field. It only lasted for a short time and with a gentle pop, it was finished. We had about twenty fireworks in the box which Dorothy lit one by one. The bangers were always fun, as they flashed into ignition, their loud explosions seemed to echo around the hillside. The cross supporting our effigy eventually burnt through, our guy succumbing to the fate of the flames licking around it. Most of our fireworks ignited, but we always had a few that failed to go off. I threw them on the fire in an attempt to ignite them. Most would ignite in a shower of bright-coloured flame within the embers of the burnt wood of our bonfire.

Our fire eventually died down until there was only glowing wood coals left with a few unburnt branch ends remaining. Dorothy raked up the remnants into a small pile and we waited until all the flames had disappeared before leaving for home. Another Guy Fawkes Day had come to an end.

It was late in the evening before we got to bed, way past the time of our regular bedtime.

The next day was a schoolday and Gran had to call us several times before we got up and dressed for school. Because we were late finishing breakfast, Dorothy said she would drive us to the Rising Sun Farm to catch the school bus, to save us our regular morning walk and, possibly, miss the bus.

Mark Carlile

Chapter 5

Unwelcome Guests

Dorothy normally had a cup of tea after supper and listened to the six o'clock news, which lasted for fifteen minutes, before going out to the cow stalls to do the milking. After the news, I listened to a fifteen-minute program called 'Dick Barton Special Agent', which was broadcast on BBC Light. That program did not come in very well on our radio. Sometimes I had to adjust the radio aerial to hear it as the signal was so weak. Because the reception was often very poor I would sit next to the radio with my ear right up tight to the speaker. Occasionally I couldn't get it at all. The program followed the exploits of ex-commando Dick Barton and his two friends, Snowy and Jock, as they solved crimes, escaped from danger and saved England from disaster.

It was a warm spring evening in May. Just after listening to my program, I opened the front door and sat on the step reading a comic. Tinker came to join me when he heard the front door open and laid on the garden pathway in front of me.

Noreen was in the dining room playing with her dolls. Gran was busy in the scullery washing the supper dishes.

Mark Carlile

When I looked up from my comic, I noticed two robins digging for worms in the garden. They did not seem to be having much success, and then one robin pulled a really long worm out of the ground and immediately, the other robin came over and tried to snatch it away and a fight started. From out of nowhere a magpie, a bird that robs other birds' nests, swooped down and tried to take the worm away from the robins, but the robins were not going to give it up. It was interesting to watch. The robins were losing the fight and about to lose their meal. Tinker looked up to see what all the squawking was about. I picked up a small stone from the garden path, threw it at the magpie and it hit it on the tail feathers and broke up the fight. The magpie flew up into the trees in the lane and one of the robins seized the opportunity to grab the worm and fly off with it. The other robin stood looking dejected.

Gran came out a little while later and said she could hear a buzzing sound coming from the living room.

"I can't find out where it's coming from." she said. "Do you have anything in the living room that could be buzzing, Michael?"

"No, I don't," I replied.

I went into the living room with Gran to see if I could hear the buzzing.

"Can you hear it?" Gran asked.

"Yes I can," I replied.

Noreen had joined us and she could also hear it. We searched the room, looking under the couch and armchairs, behind bookcases and cabinets, but couldn't find out where the buzzing was coming from. Gran went over to the fireplace and sat on the hearth to contemplate what to do.

"I think it is coming from the fireplace. Come and listen."

We walked over to where Gran was sitting and listened.

"I think you're correct," I said, "it seems to be coming from the chimney."

Unwelcome Guests

Gran bent over and tried to look up the chimney, but couldn't see anything. I had a look also and was able to look right up the chimney but couldn't see anything either. The buzzing was not very loud and was constant without variation.

"Let's go outside and see if there is something up on the roof," Gran said.

She walked through the dining room and out the front door. We followed her outside and watched as she went down the garden path far enough to look up and see the roof. She turned and looked at the roof but couldn't see anything. Then she said, "Oh my lord, look!" Noreen and I went down the path to where Gran was standing and looked up.

"The chimney," she said. "Look at the chimney."

The chimney was covered in a black blob of something.

"What is it?" I asked.

"Its bees," Gran replied. "A swarm of bees. If they get in the house, oh my goodness."

We followed Gran back to the front door, and she turned and said, "We have to block off the chimney to stop them coming in the house."

Gran grabbed a pile of old newspapers from the window seat in the dining room and a pillowcase from the linen cupboard. At the fireplace in the living room, she started crumpling up the sheets of newspapers to stuff into the pillowcase. Noreen and I helped her crumple up the newspaper to fill the pillowcase. When the pillowcase was full of paper she pushed it up the chimney. Then she got a rug from the couch and we helped her tape it up to cover the fireplace opening.

"There, that should stop those little devils from getting in the house."

Gran went out to the cow stalls where Dorothy was busy milking to tell her what had happened. Dorothy had no idea how to get rid of the bees and neither did Gran. Dorothy said she would contact one of our neighbours when she finished the milking to see if he had any suggestions on how to make the bees move on. Dorothy came in after milking and had her usual cup of tea and a biscuit. She had already been down the garden to look at the swarm of bees on the chimney.

"I have never seen anything like that before. I'll drive up to Bill Carter's farm and get his opinion on what to do. Bill is a bit of an expert on many things. I believe he has a beehive in his garden and he may be able to offer some advice."

When Dorothy returned, she said that Bill thought the bees would probably move on in the morning. He said that if the queen is old and perhaps not the strongest flyer, she probably stopped for a rest before continuing the search for a new home.

The next day was a Saturday and when Noreen and I got up and made our way to the dining room for breakfast in our dressing gowns, Gran said the bees were gone.

"Thank goodness they left, I was afraid they were going to come down the chimney and into the house."

Our unwelcome guests never did return.

Chapter 6

Springtime

On Saturday morning it was raining, and the wind was starting to pick up. It wasn't a heavy rain, just enough to prevent Noreen and me from doing anything outside. The sky looked threatening with heavy, black clouds starting to appear in the west. The early morning weather forecast was predicting that a bad storm was moving in with thunder and lightning and very high winds.

"They have also issued a storm warning to shipping in the English Channel for force ten winds," Gran said.

After we finished breakfast we decided that as it was raining and probably wouldn't stop, we would play in the hay barn for a while. The hay barn was attached to the end of the house and was full of small rectangular bales, small enough that they can be handled by one person without machinery. Each hay bale was held together with two wraps of binder twine and could be moved or lifted by the twine.

"You children go and clean your teeth before going outside," Gran reminded us.

She always made certain we cleaned our teeth in the morning and evening. We didn't bother to wash our face which we normally did before going to school as Saturday evening was sometimes our bath night.

Mark Carlile

When we went in the hay barn, Tinker jumped up from where he was lying on a bed of loose hay to welcome us. He always liked our company and often joined in with what we were doing. The hay barn was open at one end, to allow a tractor to enter to fill the barn, and there was also a large opening at the front to allow access by a tractor. The roof of the hay barn was made of corrugated steel sheet.

When the barn wasn't completely full, Noreen and I often built tunnels with the bales that led to secret rooms at the back of the barn. As it was raining, we spent several hours lifting bales and moving them around to add to the tunnels we had previously built. Sometimes, a binder twine holding the bale together would become loose and come off. Dorothy often scolded us for playing with the bales because when a bale fell apart it made it difficult for her to move and transport the bale to the cowshed.

We could hear the rain becoming heavier as it pounded on the steel roof. Water was running off the sloped roof and cascading to the ground like a waterfall at the front entrance to the barn. We could hear the distant rattle of thunder now and again as the storm approached, and the wind was starting to increase. It was time to go in as it was probably near lunchtime and we were getting hungry.

As we made a dash along the garden path to the front door in the lashing rain, a sudden gust of wind blew a flowerpot off the garden wall and into the flower bed below. Trees in the lane were bent over from the force of the wind gust, leaves were flying in the air. We burst through the front door and quickly slammed it shut against the rain and wind. After we removed our Wellingtons and put them on the mat at the door, we sat on the floor beside the fireplace to warm up and dry off. We were a little wet, but would soon dry off in front of the fire that Gran had lit to provide some heat in the dining room on this chilly morning.

Springtime

The aroma of fresh baking was drifting in from the scullery. Judging from the rattle of pots and pans Gran was obviously hard at work making something.

"What are you making?" Noreen shouted. "It smells really good."

"Nothing you would like," Gran replied.

"What is it?" Noreen asked again.

"Chocolate cake," came the reply.

"Can we have some?" Noreen shouted back as she got up and went into the scullery.

"No, not now, it will spoil your lunch. Besides, it isn't finished. After lunch you can have some."

Noreen put her finger into a bowl of chocolate icing on the counter and put it into her mouth.

"Leave it alone, Noreen," Gran told her. "If you want to help, give that icing a stir for me."

Gran was a really good cook and loved to make all sorts of things. In the summer, she would send us out with containers to pick blackberries from the hedgerows. We knew where the bushes were in the fields up the lane, generally eating a few as we picked and filled the containers. Returning with dark red blackberry juice stains on our faces and hands. Gran made blackberry pie, and blackberry and apple pie because we had lots of apples from our orchard. We also picked raspberries and gooseberries from the garden for her. She made the berries into pies and bottled some in glass jars for use in the winter.

She often made Yorkshire pudding for dinner, which Noreen and I did not like very much unless we could smother it in gravy. She made it in a large baking pan and cut it up into squares to serve, which was the traditional way of making it. When Gran was a young girl she lived in Truro, Cornwall. At age 19 in 1905, she won first prize for butter and cream making. She was awarded a silver teapot on a stand with a burner below the pot to keep the tea warm. The teapot tilted forward on the stand to pour the tea. She had it proudly displayed on a shelf in the sitting room and often polished it to keep it from tarnishing.

"What's for lunch Gran?" Noreen asked.

"Vegetable and rabbit soup with Yorkshire pudding," she replied.

Dorothy came in at 12:30 p.m. for lunch. She had been working in the cow stalls all morning, doing some repairs and a thorough cleanup as it was too wet to do anything outside.

Every now and again we could hear the wind whistling around the house and rattling a steel roof sheeting that had come loose in the wind on one of the cow sheds. The thunder was becoming more frequent, and louder as the storm approached. The rain lashed the window panes in the dining room and living room, rattling some of the loose panes every time the wind gusted. We were starting to hear the occasional crack and see the flash of lightning as it lit up our dining room. The room got darker and darker.

Dorothy pulled a chair up in front of the fire to warm up. As the heat penetrated her clothing, vapour drifted from her damp clothes.

"What did you two kids do this morning?" she asked.

"We played in the hay barn," I replied.

"I hope you didn't destroy any of the bales."

Noreen and I looked at one another for a brief second before I answered "No, we didn't."

Gran started to lay the table and said we were to sit up because lunch was ready. During lunch, Dorothy said she was going to look into the cost of installing a water tank so that we would have running water in the house. She said we had saved a little money from the milk cheques and we may be able to afford it this summer.

After our soup and Yorkshire pudding, Gran served us a slice of the chocolate cake she had made that morning along with custard and clotted cream. I loved chocolate cake and clotted cream and both Noreen and I asked for seconds when we finished our first piece.

After lunch, Dorothy went back out to finish the work she had been doing in the cow stalls. The rain was heavier now, and the thunder and lightning more frequent.

For part of the afternoon, Noreen and I played under the table. We hung rugs from the tabletop with weights on the top of the rugs to stop them falling. We used four rugs, one for each side of the table which created a little room beneath the table. Because it was already dark in the dining room as a result of the storm, it was very dark under the table. We often played under the table when the weather was bad, simulating camping in a tent. I didn't have a tent, but sometimes asked Gran if we could get one.

"We'll get a tent one day," she would say.

I think she stored this idea for a birthday gift.

The thunder was gradually getting louder and the lightning more violent. Gran said you could measure the distance of the storm from our house by counting the seconds between the thunder and lightning flash.

Dorothy came back in at 3:30 p.m. as she couldn't find anything more to do inside the sheds. Working outside in this bad weather was out of the question. She sat by the fire with a cup of tea to warm up, then spent the remainder of the afternoon until suppertime with paperwork.

The storm peaked just before three o'clock with thunderclaps that resonated throughout the house. The flashes of forked lightning crisscrossed the darkened sky in violent flashes of beauty, danger and electrical charges. Gran told us not to get too near the window as we watched the lightning display and the fierce wind blowing the trees in the lane, scattering leaves high into the sky. When we went to bed that evening, after our weekly bath in the tin tub, I lay in bed listening to the comforting sound of rain lashing the window behind my bed and wind blowing in the trees in the lane until I drifted off to sleep.

On Sunday morning the storm had passed over. All that remained was a light wind, and the damage left behind. Tree branches and leaves were scattered about in the lane and fields as remnants of the force of nature.

It was Noreen's morning job on the weekend to release the bantams from their coop, feed them and collect their eggs. The bantam coop was in a nearby field up the lane. I accompanied Noreen up the lane on this Sunday morning, picking up the tree branches that had been torn off during the storm and threw them onto the hedge. I opened the wooden five-bar gate into the field and re-latched it, after Noreen had gone through with her pail of corn in hand. The coop and wired-in run was just inside the gate and didn't look as if it had sustained any storm damage. Noreen unlatched the door of the coop, and the bantams immediately rushed out into their run as Noreen scattered corn on the ground for them to eat. One of the cocks jumped up on Noreen's arm as he often did and ate out of the pail, as she scattered the corn and filled up the corn trough. He would never do that to me if I fed the bantams, only Noreen for some reason. He obviously did not trust me.

"Not many eggs today," Noreen said when she collected the eggs. "Perhaps they were disturbed by the storm."

We generally fed the bantams in the early evening after supper on weekdays, and Noreen and I would sometimes lock them in their coop in the evening. We had to make sure they were all safely in the coop and the door securely locked in case Reynard the fox paid a visit. If a fox got in, it would kill them all, generally by ripping their heads off.

Foxes are normally nocturnal, hunting under the cover of darkness, but if really hungry they will search for prey during the daytime as well. We had chickens in our garden that wandered around the garden during the day. They were locked up in their coop at night, but if one or two did not come back to the coop at night, we didn't worry about the fox getting them. Tinker was in the barn and would chase away a fox if one was sneaking around.

During one of our lessons at school we were taught about plants, shrubs, flowers and trees. The teacher, Mr. Pinkney, brought in samples of some of the wildflowers and shrubs he talked about, handing them around for each pupil to examine. I was familiar with many of them because I lived on a farm, but some I had never heard of before.

On the way home, as Noreen, Derek Boilen and I walked along the old Roman road after being dropped off by the school bus, we stopped to pick whortleberries in the hedgerows. My teacher had briefly talked about them today, but Noreen and I had been picking them for a year or two. There were only a few places where we found them growing. They were very small berries, much like blackcurrants in size and required a lot of time to pick. We generally got a handful and walked along eating them on our walk along the road.

We walked up Derek's driveway with him and said goodbye as we came to his farm house. At the end of the driveway, we climbed the five-bar gate and made our way down the steep cow path in the common. Bucehayes Cottage could be seen down the hill to our left with smoke curling up from the chimney, and the thatched roof of Mr. Manley's cottage ahead of us, down the hill in the distance.

Further down the hill, Noreen noticed that our bantam coop and their run was just visible off to our left. We had not noticed it before, possibly because of cloud cover. As we approached Mr. Manleys cottage, we noticed that he was out in his yard splitting logs with an axe. He was rarely outside when we came home. Mr. Manley knew we sometimes walked down the common and through his yard on our way home from school, as Dorothy had mentioned it one day when she was talking to him. As we approached, he looked up and greeted us with a smile, then asked if we would like some orange juice and a biscuit. We had never really spoken to him before, except for a quick hello and a wave as we passed by his cottage. I looked at Noreen for response but she just looked back and shrugged, so I said "alright" and we followed Mr. Manley into his cottage.

A log fire was burning in the large stone fireplace and his sitting room smelt of smoke. Mr. Manley told us to take a seat and said he would get the juice and biscuits. I looked around the room and noticed several framed photographs of people and one of Mr. Manley, standing beside a horse that was hitched to a brightly painted Romany caravan. It looked like the caravan in his yard. He soon came back with a tray with two glasses of orange juice and some chocolate biscuits on a plate. He put the tray down on a small table that he placed in front of us and said to help ourselves. Mr. Manley had dark skin and the wrinkled face of a person who had spent a lot of time outdoors in the elements, similar to a farmer. He had long grey hair, with a few dark streaks in it and a short stubbly grey beard. A red plaid shirt was tucked into his baggy trousers and a blue neck scarf was knotted loosely around his neck.

He asked us about school, what we were being taught and what sports we did at school. He said he was once a traveller with his caravan and horse 'Dandy', but those days were long since gone, as now he enjoyed a more settled life in his cottage. Gran normally had supper ready at five o'clock, Noreen told him, and so after we finished our orange juice and chocolate biscuits, we said we had to go. He was a pleasant old man who seemed to enjoy talking to us and making us welcome. We realised that we had no cause to fear him or not to talk to him and be his friend. From that day on, we would often talk to him at his front gate if he was in his yard, or when we passed through his yard on the way home from school.

Gran asked why we were so long coming home after the bus dropped us off.

"We stopped to pick whortleberries on the Roman road," Noreen replied, "and then, Gypsy Manley asked us to come into his cottage for orange juice and biscuits just as we walked into his yard, after coming down the common."

"I was wondering why you were so late home. That was good of Gypsy Manley to do that. I hope the whortleberries and biscuits don't spoil your appetite for supper."

Dorothy had eventually decided that she would get the water supply run into the kitchen. It was a big job and would be costly, but would be much better for Gran as she wouldn't have to carry buckets of water in from the well. A surveyor and a construction contractor came to Post Farm one day to see if water could be found in a suitable location to provide a gravity flow to the farm, and to estimate the cost. The surveyor found water in the lower field near where we built our Guy Fawkes bonfire. The contractor would have to drill a well and see if there was sufficient flow for our needs. While we were at school the following week, the contractor drilled a well and didn't have to go very deep before he found a good flow that was more than enough for us. He said he would have to construct a small wooden pump house above the well and install a petrol-driven pump. The water would be pumped up the hill to a concrete tank he would construct on the hillside above the cowsheds in our yard. The water would then flow by gravity to a tap in our scullery. Dorothy said the contractor would be starting work next week.

The following week when we came home from school, I went down to the lower field after supper to see what the contractor had done. A wooden pump house had been built, and a pump and motor were sitting on a wooden platform on the floor inside. A trench had been dug from the pump house. It ran across the field and through a gap in the hedge which they had dug out, then up the hillside a little way. There was a little machine sitting by the trench.

The following day when I came home from school, I went down to the lower field again after supper to see if any more work had been done on the water line. A blue pipe had been laid in the trench, and the trench with the pipe in it went all the way up the hill until it was high on the hill behind the cow sheds. I asked Dorothy what they would do next. She said they would dig out the hillside in preparation for the concrete water tank which they would construct, but that wouldn't be until the following week.

I was intrigued with what they were doing and had many questions, but the contractor had always left for the day before I came home from school. I told my school friends about what was being done at our farm, but as most of them lived in Honiton they couldn't understand why we didn't have water in our house, or a toilet, the same as everyone in Honiton.

Every evening after supper I would take a walk with Tinker and see how our new water system was progressing, sometimes Noreen would come with me. The construction crew had dug out a big step in the hillside and had laid out a wooden framework inside the cut-out. There was a huge pile of dirt next to the cut-out, some of the dirt had been spread out across the field I noticed. All very intriguing. The trench with the blue pipe laid in it that came up the hillside from the pump house had not been filled in. No further work was done for two days as it had started raining, and the ground was wet and muddy where they had been working. Dorothy said they would not be back until the weather improved. On Monday, the sun came out and after supper I noticed that the pile of dirt had gone. The dirt had been spread out across the field and all that remained was a small pile of stones. The framework inside the cut-out now looked like a box with no top, and lots of steel rods were in the sides and bottom of the box.

On Tuesday after supper I took my little red cart up the lane to Gypsy Manley's gate and rode it down the lane. I had made three runs, trying to see if I could go further down the lane each time. Tinker came out from the garage from where he was lying down behind the car and joined me as I ran up the lane with the cart, for my fourth run.

"Come on Tinker," I yelled as I ran up the lane, Tinker running beside me and barking with excitement. Suddenly, Tinker darted between my legs. I tripped and fell forward, face first onto the hard surface of the lane. I let go of the cart which ran backwards down the hill and into the ditch. I picked myself up and quickly realized that I had cut my face quite badly. Blood was running down my chin and onto the front of my chest and shirt. My lip and chin was starting to sting and felt really bad. I touched my upper lip to see how bad it was, and when I looked at my fingers they were covered in blood. I walked back to the house and as I entered the dining room through the front door, Gran was just clearing away the supper dishes. She looked at me and said, "Oh my goodness. What happened?"

"Tinker tripped me," I said.

"I am sure he didn't mean to do it," Gran replied.

She grabbed a cloth from the scullery and told me to hold it up to my mouth and go into the washroom while she got some warm water in a bowl. She bathed my mouth and wiped away the blood and dirt from the cuts and said I had cut myself quite badly above my upper lip, also below my lower lip on the left side of my mouth. After cleaning the cuts she put iodine on them which stung and made me flinch. I held a cloth to the cuts for quite a while before the bleeding stopped. Gran put a plaster on both cuts and said to be really careful I do not knock them or the bleeding could start again. I stayed inside for the rest of the evening as I didn't feel like looking at the progress of our water system that evening. When I went to school the following day, my friends wanted to know what had happened to my face. "Our dog did it," I said, "but he was just playing around with me. He's a killer if he doesn't like you, he keeps away robbers from our farm. He's a good dog really and didn't intend to hurt me."

I didn't tell them I fell on my face.

It was several days later before I went up to see how the work was progressing with our water tank. The tank was finished, looking like a large concrete box with a steel hatch in the middle with a lock on it. A big pile of wood lay near the tank. A trench running down the hill from the tank to the side of the cowsheds had been dug in the ground and a blue pipe lay in the bottom. Dorothy said that the contractor only had one more day of work to finish our water system.

When I came home from school the next day, Gran said the water system was finished and she now had a water tap in the scullery. She said it would be several days before the water tank filled up, and she had to run the water to flush out the system before we could use it for drinking water. She said she could only use it for washing clothes and doing dishes until the tank was flushed out and filled up.

It was exciting to have running water and was something new to us. It would save Gran a lot of work.

John Sangster lived on a neighbouring farm and generally gave Dorothy a helping hand at haymaking time. He was a tall well-built man. The first time I met him was when he was out shooting one evening. Dorothy gave him permission to shoot rabbits on our farm, so if he was nearby he generally dropped off a rabbit or two for Gran.

I remember one warm evening when Gran, Noreen and I were sitting outside on the front step and Tinker started barking.

"I wonder what he's barking at," Gran said.

Springtime

A few minutes later John Sangster came through the gate from the orchard, crossed the yard and came to the front door where we were sitting. He had his dog with him, an Irish setter which immediately made friends with Tinker after a lot of sniffs and jockeying around. John had his gun under his arm and a rabbit in his left hand, which he handed to Gran.

"Thank you, John," Gran said. "Are you sure you don't want to keep it, you only have one."

"No that's alright. I'll probably get one or two more on the way home. There seems to be a lot of rabbits in the field below your orchard."

John unloaded his gun and put the bullet he took out into his jacket pocket. I had always been fascinated by guns and quizzed John about the one he was carrying, and the bullets it used.

"It is a single shot twenty-two."

"Do you have a bullet I could have?" I asked.

"I don't have a spent shell casing," he replied, "but if you don't mind a loud bang, I could fire a shot into the ground and give you the spent casing."

"I don't mind," I said, looking at Gran to see if she objected. She didn't.

"You may want to cover your ears when I fire this," John said, as he loaded his gun and pointed it towards the ground in front of him and fired.

It did make a loud bang which startled the dogs, and the chickens in the garden started clucking for a few seconds. John ejected the bullet casing and handed the little brass casing to me.

"Thanks John."

"Do you collect bird's eggs?" he asked.

"No, I don't."

"I've been collecting them for a number of years. If you come by my farm one day, I will show you my collection. I have a set of tools for blowing out the yoke so that only one hole has to be put in the egg, rather than one at each end."

Mark Carlile

John stayed and chatted for a little while longer and then left because he wanted to shoot more rabbits before the light faded. He often stopped in to give Gran a rabbit which she really appreciated.

Several weeks later Dorothy drove over to John's farm to see if he could help her dig a silage pit in the top field. She asked Noreen and me if we would like to go along for the ride. We had never been to his farm before so we both decided to go.

After John and Dorothy had a chat about the work she wanted help with, John showed me part of his collection of birds' eggs. He had them in a wooden tray that was divided up into little compartments with one egg in each compartment sitting on a bed of cotton wool. Each egg was identified on the side of the compartment. The eggs were very different in size and colour, some round and some like a chicken egg in shape.

He also showed me his swan's egg which was in its own little wooden box carefully packed in a nest of cotton wool to protect it. It was a very large egg but not very colourful. He said he had to swim out to the nest which was in a small pond. He had to wait for the swan to leave the nest before he could swim out, tuck an egg inside his shirt and swim back. He said swans can be very vicious, and could easily break an arm with the flap of one of their very powerful wings.

He also showed me a kestrel's egg, which was brown, with irregular shaped dark brown spots. I told him that after seeing his collection I would start saving eggs. He had duplicates of a few of his eggs that he gave me to get started, which included the eggs of a kestrel, wood pigeon, robin and sparrow, and a few others. John placed the eggs into a box with cotton wool around them, so that they wouldn't break on our way home.

He also showed me his blowing kit, which was in a polished wooden box with each tool in its own velvet lined cutout in the box. He explained what each tool was used for and demonstrated how he blows out the egg by making one small hole in the side of the egg. He said I could blow mine by making two holes with a pin, one at each end so that I can blow in one end and blow the yoke and egg white out the other end.

John really got me interested in collecting birds' eggs. It was something I could do that didn't require any money to do. On the way home in the car, I kept the box of eggs cradled on my lap to prevent the eggs from breaking on the bumpy ride home along the twisty country lanes. When I got home, Gran was busy knitting as she did quite often in the evenings. I slipped off my Wellingtons at the door and rushed over to show her my little box of eggs.

"They are very pretty colours," she remarked, and wanted to know the bird's name for each egg.

"Now I will be able to go bird nesting tomorrow," I told her.

I had a new hobby, thanks to John Sangster, that would give me many hours of enjoyment as I walked the lane and fields of our farm.

Mrs. Richard at Bowood Farm raised pigs and had advertised in the local newspaper that she had piglets for sale. Bowood Farm was about half a mile along the lane from Post Farm. One evening after Dorothy had finished milking, she walked up to Bowood Farm to see Mrs. Richard about buying a piglet to raise for eventual slaughter so that we would have our own pork and bacon. Dorothy purchased a piglet and arranged to pick it up in about three weeks' time after it had been weaned from its mother. This would give her time to make a run and a house for it to live in.

During Dorothy's conversation with Mrs. Richard, Mrs. Richard mentioned that she taught music and gave piano lessons. Dorothy told Gran about it when she returned home that evening.

Gran had a Velbeak piano in the living room but didn't play the piano. Dorothy had taken lessons when she was a teenage girl. After Gran found out that Mrs.

Mark Carlile

Richard taught the piano, she suggested that Noreen and I take lessons after the clocks changed and the evenings were lighter. She didn't want us taking lessons in the winter because it would be dark earlier, and she didn't want us walking the lane in the dark or bad weather.

The little piglet arrived one day when we were at school and was running around his enclosure beside the chicken house when we returned home in the afternoon. Noreen and I noticed him just as we approached the front door and we went down the garden to see him. He was a cute little animal with big ears and flat pink nose and danced around playfully as we approached his run. Noreen reached over the wire netting of his run and scratched his back, which he seemed to enjoy and made little snorting sounds.

"What shall we call him?" Noreen asked. "We have to give him a name."

"What about 'Snort'," I suggested, "because he makes little snorting sounds."

"No, I don't like that," she replied. "I think we should call him 'Chuggy'."

"Alright, that would be a good name for him." So Chuggy it was.

When we were having supper that evening Noreen told Dorothy that we had decided to call our piglet 'Chuggy'.

"Yes, that would suit him," Dorothy said. "I like that. You two will have to take turns in feeding him in the evenings after supper and making sure he has water."

Chuggy was always pleased to see us in the evenings and would come racing up to the wire pen where we stood. He snorted and squealed and loved to have his back rubbed. The part of the garden where Dorothy had his pen was full of weeds before he arrived, but after a few months he had most of it dug up. With his snout to the ground he would push away the soil in search of a thistle root or other tasty morsels. He quickly put on weight and it wasn't long before we noticed quite a difference in his size. When Noreen and I went up to Bowood Farm for our music lesson, Mrs. Richard often asked how our pig was doing.

"It won't be too long before you have your own bacon."

We dreaded the thought that Chuggy would be cut up for bacon and roasts but knew that one day it was destined to happen.

Now that I had the new hobby of collecting birds' eggs, I would look for nests everywhere I went. I watched for birds flying out of their nests from the hedgerows on the way to school, also on our return home across the common to Gypsy Manley's cottage.

There were curlews on most commons near the farm and we often heard their lonesome call. It is an unmistakable plaintive call 'curl-leee,' from which the name is derived. Their nests are hard to find. When the curlew feels threatened, it runs away from the nest camouflaged in the long grass or ferns before taking flight. Because of this, it is very hard to locate the curlew's nest. When we were bringing the cows in from our common on weekends, I often heard them and saw them fly up, but never did find a nest — but it wasn't for the lack of trying.

I found a number of pigeons' nests in the wood alongside our lower field but many were old nests with no eggs. Others were sometimes difficult to get to especially if high up in a tree. I was good at climbing but sometimes they were just too high up. I eventually got my pigeon's egg which was in a tree that was quite easy to climb. I had to climb down with the egg intact so that was the other consideration. If the tree was too difficult to climb, I ran the risk of breaking the egg on my descent.

I found a number of nests of robins and thrushes in the hedgerows, they were quite easy to find. If the bird only had two eggs, I only took one; if more than two

Mark Carlile

I often took two in case I broke one blowing it. Most robins and thrushes had a number of eggs so I took two.

We were wandering in the woods on the top of the hill above our yard when I spotted a nest in a tree. It wasn't a pigeon because they are generally flat and very rudimentary. The tree looked like I would be able to climb it but the nest was quite high up.

"Be careful, Michael," Noreen said. "You don't want to fall and hurt yourself."

I started to climb and managed to get about halfway before taking a rest. It looked like I would make it but some of the tree limbs were not very thick, and I had to think about coming down again. The wind was blowing which caused the tree to sway which did not help. I managed to get within arm's length and put my hand in the nest. After that difficult climb, I found it had about five eggs. Thank goodness I thought. I took two eggs and popped them into my shirt pocket. The eggs were pale blue with dark blotches which I could not immediately identify. Now all I had to do was get down without falling or breaking the eggs. I took my time on the descent, but the wind had increased which did not help and several times when my foot slipped I could not help wondering if I would make it. In addition to the wind, it had also started to rain making the branches slippery. I was over halfway down and my face and hands were feeling really cold and were starting to get wet. My foot slipped sideways on a thin wet branch and I thought I would fall, but I managed to regain balance when I took a desperate step down to a lower branch. I thought how lucky I was when I made it to ten feet from the ground where the lower branches were thicker and more plentiful. Noreen watched me all the way down. I showed Noreen the two eggs and asked her to carry one home.

"What are these eggs?" she asked.

"I don't know, I will have to look it up in my bird book when we get home."

Springtime

The rain was increasing, and we were both a little wet and cold with still a trek through the woods and down the hill to our farm yard. By the time we reached the edge of the woods where there was a little shelter from the rain, we could see that it was raining quite hard across the open field. We had no rain wear whatsoever. This would result in us getting quite wet as we walked as fast as possible down the steep open field and past the water tank to the yard. We would also need to be very careful not to slip and fall on the slippery wet grass and break the eggs.

The top of the hill was reasonably flat, so we ran across that part and slowed to a walk at the steep slope just above the water tank. It was difficult to prevent our feet from slipping on the wet grass on the steep hillside. At the water tank, the rougher area where the water line was buried that had not grown over with grass gave much better grip than the wet grass. Our hair and clothing were soaked by the rain. With water running down our faces, we were both cold and very uncomfortable. Upon reaching the yard, I opened the wooden gate, and we raced across the yard and along the path to the front door. After bursting in, it was good to find a roaring fire burning in the hearth. Gran was sitting in her armchair knitting.

"If you're wet you better change into dry clothes before you catch your death of cold."

We went up to our bedrooms, found dry clothing, and then returned to the fireplace with a towel to dry our hair. Noreen had thick black wavy hair which took her a little while to dry. My brown hair, which was short, dried in a few seconds. After we warmed up, I got my bird book, which Gran had given me, and started searching to try to identify the eggs. It took a lot of page turning and narrowing down until I looked under jackdaw. There was a little picture of a jackdaw's nest with eggs in it. It seemed to match the eggs we came back with and the nest looked like the one in the tree that I had climbed. I decided that I had found two Jackdaw eggs.

When Dorothy saw me blowing the eggs one evening, she said I was cruel because I was killing birds by taking their eggs. Perhaps it was, thinking back on it, but I didn't take any notice of her at the time. Dorothy was very protective of animals and birds.

Dorothy was starting to prepare the top field for planting seed. She had plowed the ground with her little Ferguson tractor which took many hours over several days. It was a long process for her and the little Ferguson was not particularly comfortable to ride on for hour after hour. Vibration from the tractor came up through the seat, and the oily smell of the tractor's exhaust sometimes blew back into her face, thanks to the wind. She often got backache from sitting for so long and had to shut the tractor down and take a rest for a while. She would stand by the tractor and pour herself a cup of coffee from the thermos, eat a couple of biscuits or piece of cake if Gran had any available when she had packed her snack and made coffee for her.

After plowing the field, Dorothy broke up the plowed ground with a disc. It was a little faster than the plow but still required many boring hours of sitting on the tractor. Noreen and I often rode on the tractor with her for company on weekends. Only one of us would ride as space was limited. Dorothy didn't particularly like us riding with her because she was always concerned that we may fall off. Noreen was riding today, so I took the opportunity to search the hedgerows for birds' nests, but didn't find any.

As we were next to our common, I decided to sit and watch for a curlew to fly up and then go and look for the nest. The gorse was starting to flower. Many of the bushes were covered with yellow flowers that gave off a sweet aroma to combine with the musty smell of bracken. The hill seemed alive with the chatter of songbirds that were attracted to the flowering gorse.

Springtime

Now and again I would hear the distant plaintive cry of a curlew as I sat in the warmth of the sun's rays surveying the hillside. I loved the common as it gave me a sense of freedom with its natural beauty where everything was alive and flourishing, where rabbits, fox, badgers and mice wandered in a natural non-restrictive freedom.

Our cows were on the hillside today. I could see two or three of them slowly ambling along one of the many cow paths that criss-crossed the hillside. Tinker came to join me and must have been chasing rabbits on the hillside for a while as he was covered in sticky buds. I started pulling them out, but some were so tangled in his thick coat that I could not get them out. They would have to be cut out when we returned home.

I could hear the little Ferguson droning away in the distance as it went backwards and forwards across the field. Suddenly I heard it stop and a few minutes later, it started up again and the sound of its engine grew louder. I assumed that Dorothy had finished for the day and was on her way to the gate to the common with the tractor.

I walked over to the gate to find Noreen holding the gate open and the tractor coming through. After Noreen closed the gate, Dorothy turned off the tractor and climbed down.

"Would you children drive the cows down out of the common, and I will meet you with the tractor at the entrance of Snodwell Lane. I see that Tinker is with you, I wondered where he had gone."

Dorothy climbed back on the tractor and started it up as Noreen, Tinker and I walked over to the cow path that led down and across the common. We could see two cows from our vantage point and knew that the others would not be far away as they tended to stick together. By the time we walked down to them along the well-trodden path, we could see two more lying down and the others behind some tall bracken. With Tinker's help, we soon had them moving downhill and across the common towards Snodwell Lane where there was a gate to drive them into the lane. It was a slow process, but eventually we reached the gate where Dorothy was waiting with the gate open. The lead cow, a Guernsey named Jinx, knew where she had to go and the others followed her the short distance in single file to Post Lane where she instinctively made a left down the lane. When we arrived at the entrance to the farm, Jinx made a left along the back of the house and over to the dairy where the door was open for them to go inside. Each cow knew their stall and made their way over and into their stall as they had done many times before. Noreen tied them to the rail and came back out and closed the door.

I went into the garden to give Chuggy his nighttime feed and replenished the water in his water trough which was completely dry. He squealed and snorted when he saw me coming and rushed up to the fence to greet me. He was a thirsty, hungry little pig, and he was gaining lots of weight. He started wolfing down the feed I had just given him as fast as he could. I reached over the fence and scratched his back and left him to his meal.

When I opened the front door Gran was just laying the table for supper.

"What's for supper?" I asked. "I'm really hungry."

"Chicken with mashed potatoes, brussels sprouts and carrots."

After supper, I listened to Dick Barton Special Agent on the radio but the reception was very poor again. I had to keep my ear right up to the speaker as it was very hard to hear. Dorothy had started listening to a new radio program called The Archers. It was the story of country folk and was based in the fictional village of Ambridge. It was about the everyday lives of three farmers. Dan Archer, farmed efficiently with little money; Walter Gabriel, farmed inefficiently with little money; and George Fairbrother, a very wealthy businessman, farmed at a loss for tax purposes. The reception was much better than Dick Barton because it was on a different station. I often listened with Dorothy as did Gran and Noreen.

Later when Gran was in the scullery washing the dinner dishes, I helped her by doing the drying with a tea towel. Noreen also came to help. My birthday was in September which was several months away. I had been looking in the toy shops on our trips to Honiton and spotted an air rifle in a shop window which I thought I would really like for my next birthday. As I dried the dishes I waited for an opportune moment and asked Gran if she would get it for my birthday.

"Well, I don't know, Michael, it depends how much it costs."

"If I could have it in advance of my birthday I would have all summer to shoot some rabbits."

"The next time we go Honiton you will have to show it to me," Gran said. "I don't know if I can afford it."

I left it like that as I knew Gran would think about it as she had not said no.

After we finished helping Gran with the dishes, Noreen and I walked up the lane to feed the bantams. It was starting to get very dark mostly because of the low black clouds that were swiftly coming in, bringing rain — according to the radio. The crisp bark of a fox could be heard way off in the distance as we approached the field where the bantams were. I opened the gate and Noreen opened the pen with her bucket of feed in hand. They all came running to Noreen as she broadcast seed and filled their trough. I had a bucket of water to fill up their water container, which I washed out before refilling it with clean water. When we returned later to shut the bantams in for the night, I saw a fox running down the hill a short distance away as I opened the gate to the field.

"Did you see that fox?" I asked Noreen.

"I thought I saw something moving by that bush on the brow of the hill."

Mark Carlile

"Yes, I saw it before we went through the gate; it was a fox. He would have been in after the bantams if we didn't get here when we did."

We made sure that all the bantams were safely locked away before leaving. Just as I closed the gate I saw a fox moving along the brow of the hill.

"Let's walk over to that bush where you saw movement," I said to Noreen. "I think that fox is still there."

It was spotting with rain and a cold wind was blowing in from the east, chilling the side of my face as we walked over to the bush on the brow of the hill. We saw two foxes running down into the valley and quickly disappear into a clump of trees.

"Those crafty foxes were watching for us to go and they were going to return to get the bantams," I said to Noreen.

"Well, they are out of luck because they can't get into the bantam house."

When we got home, Dorothy had just finished milking, and was in the dining room with her usual cup of tea and some biscuits. We told her about the foxes that we saw in the bantams' field, and how they were watching for us to leave.

"Perhaps we should lock them away earlier so that they are in bed well before dark. We don't want anything to happen to them. If a fox got in he would kill them all. Lock them in at seven instead of eight," she said. "Probably that will help. It is exceptionally dark tonight because of the rain clouds coming in, which is probably why they are prowling around so early."

Not long after we returned home, the rain and wind moved in just as the radio weather station had predicted. Heavy rain started to pound on the windows. It was going to be another stormy night.

We started locking the bantams away earlier after that and did not see the foxes sneaking around again. But we did hear their familiar crisp bark once in a while, so we knew that they were still around. If only I had a gun to shoot them, but I was too young to handle a shotgun.

Dorothy still had lots of work left to prepare the top field for seeding. She spent many more hours preparing the ground and seeding, then it was up to Mother Nature to germinate the seeds with just the right amount of rain. Too much rain could be very destructive and could result in many more hours of work and a lot of additional cost, but that was the risk that every farmer took every year. Farming had it risks but farmers always picked themselves up and overcame the disasters caused by wind and rain, which was completely out of their control. Dorothy was lucky; she never had a crop destroyed by Mother Nature.

The next time we went to Honiton I persuaded Gran to come with me to look at the air rifle in the window of the toy store, the gun was no longer in the window. My heart sank as I thought they had sold it and probably didn't have another one.

"Let's go in and see if they still have it," I said to Gran. "Perhaps they just took it out of the window."

"I'm not buying it today, even if they have one, Michael."

"Alright, but we can have a look to see if they have it in the shop."

We entered the toy store and as soon as I saw the salesperson at the counter, I rushed up to him and asked if they still had the air rifle that was in the window a few weeks ago.

"We still have one," he replied, and went to the back of the store and came back with a long box with the picture of an air rifle on the top, and the word 'Diana' in big letters written beside it.

He opened the box and pulled back the packing paper to expose the rifle.

"It comes with three targets and a box of two hundred pellets. We sell boxes of five hundred pellets if you need more."

Mark Carlile

I picked up the rifle and found that it was heavier than I thought. It was a real gun so I should have expected it to be heavier than a toy.

"How much is it?" Gran asked. The salesperson looked on the side of the box.

"It is three pounds," he said. "Would you like me to wrap it up for you?"

"No thanks," Gran replied. "Perhaps we'll come back some other time."

I followed Gran out feeling very disappointed that she wouldn't buy it for me. When we were outside the shop, Gran said, "I just can't afford it, Michael. You can't expect me to buy everything you see and want, I'm not made of money. Perhaps I will have more money in September when it's your birthday. You will have to wait and see."

All the way home in the car I pondered my disappointment at not getting the rifle. It was something I really wanted. I never said any more about it to Gran. I knew I would have to wait a few more months until my birthday in September if she couldn't afford to buy it for me now.

Chapter 7

The Start of Summer

The weather was starting to improve. The days were getting longer, rain showers were less frequent, and I could often feel the warmth of the sun on my face and arms. It was a welcome change from the frequent cold days of spring that we had been experiencing over the past few months. I loved the summer months. School would finish in July. Noreen and I would have what often seemed like an endless holiday of warm weather to enjoy our freedom on the farm, doing whatever we felt like doing with no thought of school. We would not have to get up early to walk up Post Lane and along the old Roman road to catch the school bus at the Rising Sun. I would miss my school friends but during the school holidays I sometimes invited a friend to come and stay for a few days.

I asked Gran if I could have a tent, just a small tent that I could put in the garden. I was always asking her for something but generally had to wait for my birthday or Christmas. Gran found an advertisement in the newspaper for army surplus tents and they were not expensive because they wanted to get rid of them. When we next went to Honiton, we stopped in at the surplus store that was selling them. Gran bought one for me and the man at the store loaded it into the car. It looked like it was quite heavy and had one tent pole which was in two pieces which slotted together.

When we returned home, Dorothy helped Noreen and me to put it up in the field behind the cow sheds. It was a large bell tent much bigger than I really wanted. Noreen and I could not put it up on our own because it was very heavy. When it was fully erected, we could stand up inside. The location where we had it was a little sloped and not the ideal place, but the tent was too large to be put up in our garden. I didn't complain because it was so large but I would have much preferred a two-man tent. Noreen and I stored a number of our possessions inside during the summer. It was made of very heavy dark brown fabric and was very waterproof. During the summer we spent many happy hours playing in the tent and around it, acting out characters such as Robin Hood and Maid Marian, Cowboys and Indians, Snow White, and Jack in the Beanstalk.

Dorothy had a small five-acre field at the entrance to the laneway of Snodwell Farm. Every year she grew a crop of kale for animal feed in that field. It was a type of kale that grew quite tall with a thick stalk and large green leaves. When she cut the kale generally early in the morning on a weekend, Noreen and I would often help her. She had a small trailer that she hitched up to her little Ferguson tractor to collect the kale. She would park the tractor and trailer at the end of the field and cut the kale with a sickle. Noreen and I also had sickles so that we could help her cut. If there had been a recent rain, you had to be careful that the big leaves did not contain a pool of cold water hiding inside. The water could fall on your back as the kale fell to the ground after you slashed through the stalk. After cutting a row of kale, Dorothy drove the tractor and trailer along the row, stopping for Noreen and me to load the kale on the trailer.

The Start of Summer

When Dorothy fertilized the field after planting, she did it by hand from a bucket. She would walk up and down the field, hand broadcasting the fertilizer as she walked. Noreen often helped her mother do the fertilizing. Dorothy said she could generally see where Noreen had broadcast the fertilizer. The kale was generally taller in that area because Noreen broadcast more fertilizer than she did.

We often helped Dorothy with farm work, especially on weekends. We always looked forward to haymaking time because Uncle Len and some of his friends would help with the haymaking. Noreen and I would ride on the trailer as the hay was collected from the field. We had our daily duties to perform like feeding the bantams and our pig, and we often helped with getting the cows in for milking and turning them out to pasture on weekend mornings and on holidays. Dorothy could do all these daily farm activities without our help but she always worked really long hours. The little help that Noreen and I gave her helped to make her day a little shorter and easier. We never received any pocket money for our help and never expected any. Dorothy and Gran could not afford it. Helping was something we were expected to do, and we rarely complained about helping on the farm. Most of the things we helped with we enjoyed doing. We loved the few animals that we had. They were like our pets and all had names that Dorothy or Noreen and I had given them. They were like our family. Our reward was fireworks on Guy Fawkes Day, sweets when we went grocery shopping at Mrs. Clark's shop in Stockland, and sometimes an ice cream when we went to Honiton. Children at school, most of whom lived in Honiton, envied us because we lived on a farm.

"You're lucky to have all the animals you talk about, and the fields, woods and common to walk and explore. I wish I lived on a farm."

I was always a bit of a prankster. I loved to think up tricks to play on people, including Noreen, Gran and

Mark Carlile

Dorothy. If I teased Noreen or played a trick on her she sometimes told her mother.

"Don't take any notice of him, Noreen, he is just being cruel to you. He can be a little devil sometimes."

My Grandfather, whom I rarely saw because he lived and worked in Taunton, took snuff. He had little tins the snuff came in and when he thought no one was looking, he would take a pinch of the brown powder from his little snuff tin and sniff it up each nostril. Then he would sneeze and blow his nose vigorously. Strange thing to do I thought. Why would you sniff something up your nose that made you sneeze? I couldn't understand it. From sniffing the snuff, he also had a brown stain just below his nose. Gran said it was a filthy habit and a waste of money. One day when we visited him, I asked him if he had an empty snuff tin I could have. He found one on his dressing table beside his hairbrush and gave it to me. I kept the little tin in my bedside table drawer not knowing what I could use it for. It was just a little tin, the smallest tin I had ever seen, and that's the thing that intrigued me and why I kept it.

One evening during supper, I remembered the little tin and had an idea for a trick I would play on my school friends. After supper I asked Gran if I could have some cocoa. She made me a mug of cocoa and I sat at the table drinking it after Noreen went to help her mother in the cow stalls. Gran left the cocoa tin on the table after she made my drink and returned to the scullery to wash the supper dishes. I ran upstairs to my bedroom and got the little snuff tin and ran back down to the dining room to finish my cocoa. I took the lid off the cocoa tin and with the spoon that Gran had left on the table I put some cocoa in the little snuff tin, then quickly replaced the lid on the cocoa tin. Gran generally left the pepper and salt on the table because we nearly always used it for every meal. I reached for the pepper and shook a good quantity of it into the snuff tin. I was growing excited about what I was going to do. Then I mixed the contents of the snuff tin with the end of the spoon. When it was well mixed it looked just like snuff. I quickly closed the snuff tin giving it a good shake to ensure it was well mixed and put the little tin in my pocket. If Gran caught me doing this she would have asked me what I was doing and I wouldn't have had a good answer. I am sure she would have been very cross with me. I quickly rushed upstairs to my bedroom and hid the little snuff tin under some cotton wool inside my bird's egg box. I returned to the dining room and sat there finishing my cocoa and pondering my plan. Gran was still busy washing dishes in the scullery.

On Monday morning just before I left for school, I took out the snuff tin from my hiding place in the birds' egg box and slipped it into my trouser pocket.

On the way to school on the bus, I thought about the fun I was going to have with my snuff. I decided to wait until after lunch when we were all out in the playground. Our lunchtime was from twelve until one fifteen. Most of my friends and classmates finished their lunch by twelve thirty, then spent the rest of the time relaxing on the grass, playing with a ball or playing hopscotch on the playground.

I was sitting on the grass with a number of classmates when I pulled out the snuff tin.

"What's that?" Derek asked as he saw me fingering the tin.

"It's snuff," I told him. "You sniff it up your nose."

"Can I try it?" he asked.

"Yes you can," I replied, "but just take a small pinch."

I opened the tin and Derek took a pinch and sniffed it up his nose. He immediately began to sneeze violently and quickly pulled out his handkerchief and blew his nose. Several other classmates noticed what Derek was doing and wanted to try it. It was a huge prank to me as I sat there inwardly laughing at them all as they took a pinch of my snuff and started sneezing as soon as they sniffed it up their noses. If only they knew that they were sniffing cocoa and pepper up their noses. I never used that prank again but often had a secret chuckle whenever I remembered it.

I did a few silly things when I lived on the farm that got me into trouble. I should have known better, but I seemed to act without thinking of the consequences. Teasing Noreen was one of my favorite pastimes. One evening after we bathed, cleaned our teeth and climbed into bed, I decided I was going to play a prank on Noreen. We had been in bed for about fifteen minutes, and were chatting back and forward from our bedrooms which we quite often did, when I made this "Buzzzzzz" sound.

"What's that," Noreen asked.

"I didn't hear anything," I replied.

Then a few minutes later I made it again. "Buzzzzzz."

"There, did you hear it?"

"No, I didn't hear anything." I waited several more minutes and then made the sound again. "Buzzzzzz."

"There it is again," Noreen said. "Are you sure you can't hear it?"

"No," I replied again. "I can't hear anything. What does it sound like?"

"It's a buzzing sound. Are you sure you didn't hear it?"

"No," I replied again. I waited for about ten minutes and made the sound again.

"Mum," Noreen shouted for her mother. "Mum!" she shouted again.

A few minutes later her mother shouted up the stairs.

"What do you want, Noreen?"

"I keep hearing a strange noise, come up and listen."

Dorothy came up the stairs, which was right next to my bed, so I pretended I was asleep. When Dorothy entered Noreen's room which was also her mother's bedroom, she asked Noreen what sort of noise she was hearing.

"It's a buzzing sound," Noreen replied. "Listen and you'll hear it."

They both listened for the sound but of course did not hear it. Dorothy said, "It's probably Mr. Manley sawing logs, now go to sleep. Michael's asleep; if you call again you'll wake him up."

I thought that I better not do it again because I might get caught. I had my fun for the evening so I rolled over and went to sleep.

I really loved playing pranks. I would often think about them for some time before putting them into practice.

One afternoon Noreen and I were playing in the yard just outside the hay shed. We had set up a target in the yard and were shooting our bow and arrows at it. Gran was in the house and Dorothy had gone somewhere with the tractor and trailer. She had been gone for some time. I was starting to get bored with target practice and my eyes wandered to a pile of junk in the corner of the yard. An old car tire, bricks and stones, pieces of wood, empty tins, pieces of cardboard, old boots, pieces of wire netting and an old bucket. The old bucket was a little rusty and had a hole in one side where it had rusted through. I walked over to the junk pile and pulled the bucket free of the wire netting and emptied the contents — rusty nails, old hinges and old door locks — onto the junk pile. An idea flashed in my mind, I would make a fire in the bucket! There was always some hay scattered around in the hay barn that had fallen from the bales as they were loaded into and out of the barn. Sometimes Dorothy would clean it all up and use it in the pig house for bedding.

I filled the old bucket with hay and set it down outside the hay barn.

"What are you doing?" Noreen asked.

"You'll see," I replied.

Mark Carlile

I had a box of matches in my pocket which only had three or four matches in it. I had taken a few matches from a box on the fireplace mantel where Gran kept them. When Gran used the last match in the box, I asked her if I could have the box. Gran would not let us have matches to play with so this was how I got my matches.

I took out the box of matches from my pocket and struck a match which did not want to light at first. After a few attempts it lit. I bent down and put the small flame of the match to the hay in the bucket. The hay lit up immediately and, after a few seconds, flames were rising well above the bucket as the dry packed hay burned. Just as I had a good fire going inside the bucket, I heard the tractor coming down the lane. It was totally unexpected, and I didn't have enough time to put the fire out before the tractor came into the yard. Quickly, I did the first thing that entered my head. I kicked the bucket over and stood on it, thinking the fire would go out. As Dorothy entered the yard, smoke was shooting out around the upturned bucket and out of the hole in the side. Dorothy turned her head to see what we were doing and came to an abrupt stop when she saw me standing on the bucket with the smoke rising around me, getting in my eyes and making me cough.

She immediately shut the tractor down, climbed off and came running over with a look of anger on her face. She grabbed my arm and pulled me off the bucket and yelled "what do you think you are doing, you stupid, stupid boy." She kicked the bucket over and away from the hay barn as smoke swirled around us. Embers from the burning hay spewed out into the yard which she quickly stamped out with her feet. Red in the face she turned to me, still furious, and said, "You could have set the hay barn alight. What on earth do you think you are doing? Haven't you got anything better to do?"

I stood there in dismay, saying nothing, fearful of what she would say and do next as she scolded me for lighting a fire in the old bucket. I had thought it could do no harm.

Dorothy turned to Noreen who stood there watching the berating I was getting.

"Did you see what he was doing?"

"I didn't do it," Noreen replied. "It's not my fault."

"You could have stopped him, Noreen. Silly little boy."

Noreen did not reply, she could see her mother was very angry and upset so thought better of it.

Dorothy got back on the tractor and started it up and proceeded to the orchard gate. It was open, and she drove just inside the orchard and parked the trailer and unhitched it.

I realized that I had not heard the end of this, because as soon as Dorothy told Gran, I would receive another scolding. Gran would want to know where I got the matches from. I would have to think up a good answer for that.

I stayed out until it was time for supper making some new arrows for my bow. I cut small straight branches from the hedge beside Post Lane, cut them to length, removed the bark and cut a sharp point on one end and a 'V' notch in the other end for the bow string.

I wasn't looking forward to supper because I knew Dorothy would have told Gran about the fire in the bucket. I played around with Tinker until Gran shouted out the front door that it was supper time; then I went in to face the music. When I slipped off my boots at the front door, I noticed that my supper was already on the table and everyone had started eating. I swilled my hands at the sink in the scullery and dried them on a towel that Gran had hanging on the wall. As I started my supper, I wondered when Gran would say something about the fire. Everyone was eating in silence and Dorothy, as she ate, was intently studying a letter that was beside her plate. You could have cut the silence with a knife.

"Can I have some more milk?" I asked Gran.

Mark Carlile

"Yes, I'll get the jug," she replied.

She filled my glass and sat down to finish her supper. Once Dorothy had finished reading her letter she started talking to Gran about meeting the bank manager. Safe so far, I thought, maybe Gran won't mention it.

After Dorothy and Noreen finished their apple pie and cream which Gran had made, Dorothy got up to go and do the milking. She asked Noreen if she would help in the cow stalls for half an hour which she often did. Gran asked me if I would like more apple pie and cream. She knew I liked my pie and always had a second piece if it was available. She took my dessert dish and came back a few minutes later with my pie and a cup of tea for herself. As I started to eat, I was waiting for the moment she would ask about the fire I had lit. I knew it was about to come at any second.

Gran took a few sips of her tea and blew on it a few times as it was obviously very hot.

"What's this I hear about you lighting a fire in a bucket right in front of the barn door, Michael?"

"Yes, well I did it," I replied.

"What on earth were you thinking? You could have burnt the barn down and possibly this house as well. Did you not think of that?"

I did not reply, the less said the better I thought to myself.

"Where did you get the matches?" she asked.

I had to tell a white lie here because I didn't want to tell her I stole them from the box on the mantel piece.

"I found them," I replied. I did find them on the mantelpiece so it was not a complete lie, I told myself.

"Where did you find them?" Gran asked.

Now it was getting tricky. I didn't want to tell her where I really got them.

"In the roadway," I replied, which was a lie but I could not avoid it.

It was always drummed into Noreen and me that we should never lie so I felt ashamed that I had to be

The Start of Summer

untruthful. It was something I disliked doing. Perhaps God would punish me for it one day, I thought. "Make sure you never do anything like that again. I thought you had better sense than that. Always think before you consider doing anything like that, Michael. Think of the damage you could have caused."

I quickly finished the last mouthful of apple pie and cream, drained my milk glass and got up and left the table, slipped on my boots at the front door and made a hasty retreat before Gran could think of anything else.

I went to the barn, got some feed for Chuggy, a bucket of water and made my way to his run in the garden. He was pleased to see me and came snorting up to the fence as I poured feed into his trough along with some water. Then I refilled his water trough which was almost empty. As he ate, I talked to him and scratched his back which he always seemed to appreciate. He was getting really big now, and I knew that one day soon, we would be enjoying his bacon for breakfast and pork roasts for supper. It was not a nice thought, but it was a reality that I knew Noreen would have difficulty with. I returned the buckets to the barn and went to the front step to enjoy the fragrance from the garden and the warmth of the sinking sun in the western sky. Tinker came to sit with me and rested his head on my knee.

I loved the summer evenings on the farm. I could hear a pigeon cooing way off in the distance, and the occasional 'cuckoo', which was unmistakable. The cuckoo lays its eggs in other birds' nests and lets that bird hatch and rear them. In flight, the cuckoo is easily mistaken for a sparrow hawk or kestrel, my bird book said. They arrive in England in April and return to Central and Southern Africa in August. I had never seen one and only heard them way off in the distance. I did not have a cuckoo's egg in my collection. Perhaps one day I will be lucky enough to find one.

Our garden smelled beautiful with the abundance of flowers that Gran so carefully planted. She loved her garden, spending many hours planting and taking care of it. Noreen and I sometimes helped her and we each had our own little patch where we planted flower seeds and nurtured the plants as they grew and flowered.

When Noreen finished helping her mother she came to get me to help her carry water up the road for the bantams which was our nightly job of feeding them and locking them away for the night.

Dorothy was starting to prepare for haymaking. One afternoon she and Noreen walked up Post Lane and across the common to the top field to inspect the grass to see when it would be ready to mow. She carried her hook because she intended to cut some small branches from the hedge that ran alongside Post Lane to make spars. The grass was growing well because the weather had been kind with just the right amount of rain and sunshine. She estimated that in about another two weeks, weather permitting, it would be ready to mow.

Every year, Dorothy made wood spars for the hayrick. She cut lengths of thin hazel saplings from the hedge with a hook, cut them to length, sharpened both ends to a point, and made a small cut at the middle which allowed her to bend the sapling in half but not break it in two. As Dorothy cut and formed the spars, Noreen picked them up and kept them in a bundle for her mother. As she sharpened the next spar, Noreen noticed blood coming from her mother's left hand.

"Why is your hand bleeding?"

Dorothy looked at her hand and immediately saw blood pouring from her thumb.

"Oh, my gosh!" she exclaimed when she saw it, as blood dripped profusely from her left hand.

She quickly grabbed a handkerchief from her pocket and applied it to her thumb. Unbeknown to her, she had cut off the side of her thumb with the hook as she sharpened a spar to a point. Dorothy pulled the bottom of her shirt out from her trousers and wrapped her thumb with the shirt as best she could, told Noreen that she felt faint and needed to get home as quickly as possible. They made their way to the gate that opened up into Post Lane. Noreen opened the gate for her mother and closed it behind them. Noreen noticed that her mother's face had turned white, and she looked really worried.

"Are you okay?" she asked her mother as they walked down the steep hill towards the entrance of Snodwell Farm.

"I'm alright," she replied. "I'm just feeling a little faint."

Noreen held on to her mother's right arm as they made their way to the bottom of the hill past the entrance to Bucehayes Cottage and the sharp right in the lane. They still had about a ten minute walk before they reached Post Farm as she was walking quite slowly. When they reached Post Farm, Noreen opened the garden gate and they burst through the front door as Dorothy yelled, "Mother, come quickly." She sank into a dining room chair with a sigh of relief that she had made it home.

When Gran saw all the blood on Dorothy's shirt with her hand wrapped in it, she said, "What in the world happened?"

Dorothy explained what she had done and Gran immediately got a basin of water from the scullery and a cloth to clean the wound. The basin of water was soon red as Dorothy's thumb was still bleeding badly. Gran removed her hand from the water and wrapped it in a towel. She got a bottle of Iodine from a cabinet in the scullery and removed the top from the little brown bottle.

"Now this is going to sting," she said to Dorothy. "But we have to disinfect the cut."

When Gran poured on the Iodine, Dorothy nearly leapt out of the chair.

"God that stings, and it is really throbbing."

Gran bandaged the thumb after she patted it dry and then made a thumb stall out of an old pair of leather gloves. She secured the makeshift thumb stall to Dorothy's wrist with a shoe lace that she threaded through a hole in the thumb stall. Noreen and I watched intently. After Gran had finished, Dorothy said that Noreen and I would have to do the milking tonight because she could not bend her thumb on her left hand. The cows were in the lower field at the bottom of the orchard, so after supper Noreen, Tinker and I did not have far to go to bring them in for milking. We soon had them in their stalls. Dorothy cleaned their udders with warm water and a cloth using her right hand as Noreen and I sat down on our stools with a bucket for milking. Noreen often helped her mother milk, but I was a little out of practice because I only helped when Dorothy was really busy such as haymaking time.

Cows are like any other animal, they get to know who is milking them and do not appreciate different hands pulling on them. When I started, a tail swished around my back telling me to take it easy. A little later a knee kicked up almost kicking over the bucket of milk between my legs, telling me I was pulling too hard. I rested my head against the cow's belly and carried on. There is a little art in hand milking, and the cow can often tell immediately when unpractised hands are doing the milking. Noreen finished her first cow and had started her second before I finished my first. It was not a job I liked doing. I did not like the smell of cows or the smell of cow stalls, and warm milk was something that was not appealing to me. When I finished my first cow, Noreen checked to see if there was any milk left in my cow before I started on my second. It took us much longer than Dorothy would have taken but that was to be expected. While we were milking, Dorothy fed Chuggy and went up Post Lane to feed the bantams as she only needed her right hand for that. Our roles had sort of been reversed.

Noreen and I did the milking morning and night for about ten days until Dorothy's thumb healed to the point where she could bend it without opening up the nasty wound. She should have gone to the hospital for stitches as it was a large cut. She didn't go because she would have had to drive herself into Honiton as Gran did not drive. It was fortunate that we were on our summer holidays and were able to help. I was tired of getting up early in the morning as I am not normally an early riser, neither was Noreen. Dorothy was really grateful for our help and bought us both a second-hand bicycle as a thank you. We spent the next few days learning to ride and soon got the hang of it, riding up and down Post Lane. I had a few falls and scraped my leg and elbow but nothing serious.

Dorothy checked the grass in the top field and decided that it was ready to cut. She spent the next few days with the mower behind the tractor, driving up and down the field until it was all cut. She would not let us in the field while she was mowing because of the mower's sharp blades. We also had to keep Tinker at home as she didn't want him near the mower either. Just before lunchtime, we took Dorothy's lunch and a flask of coffee up to her. We sat with her on the grass at the top of the common by the Nissen hut while she ate her lunch, and we ate some chocolate biscuits that Gran packed for us. We could smell the scent of the freshly cut grass which mingled with the aroma of coffee as she poured herself a cup. It was warm in the midday sun as Dorothy relaxed for half an hour. When she returned to her mowing, we walked down the cow paths on the common, through the gate onto Snodwell Drive, down Post Lane to home. It was long days for Dorothy, from sunup to sundown, and once again, Noreen and I helped with the milking in the evenings. It was an excellent crop; the weather had been kind this year.

John Sangster had helped Dorothy excavating the pit for silage, back in the spring, as she intended to make a little silage this year. The silage pit was very near where the hayrick would be. Using the tractor with forks on the front, she brought in the green grass that was nearest to the pit and filled the pit. She could drive into the pit, dump the grass and drive back out. When she had enough grass in the pit, she poured molasses over the grass, covered the grass with a tarp and weighted it down with wooden boards and old car tires that were stored in the Nissen hut.

Dorothy took a little break for a few days after making the silage while the cut grass in the field dried in the sun, then spent several more days with help from Uncle Len and some of his friends turning the rows of cut grass with pitchforks. Noreen and I helped do this for a few hours in the afternoon, but I am not sure how much help we were because we often took breaks and eventually got tired of turning grass. It was hard backbreaking work in the hot sun, but eventually they got it all turned so that the grass could dry on the opposite side. Many farmers had machines to turn the grass but Dorothy could not afford to buy one and did not know of one she could borrow.

She had a few more days of haymaking and returned to milking in the evenings. After the evening milking she would come in and have a cup of tea but often fell asleep in the chair. Then Gran would wake her up with a fresh cup of tea because her tea had gone cold. She looked tired and exhausted from the hard work and long hours. Fortunately, she only did this in the summer and had less work to do in the winter months.

After the grass was completely dry she had to bring it in to the corner of the field near the gate to the common where she built a hayrick. Once again, Uncle Len and his friends came up in the afternoons to help her, and Noreen and I also lent a hand. Dorothy drove the tractor and trailer down the rows of dried grass, which was now hay, stopped the tractor and helped the men fork up the hay on the hay wagon. Noreen and I were on the hay wagon with wooden rakes spreading the hay evenly over the floor of the wagon. The hay gradually built up on the wagon until it was at the top of the wagon side racks. I loved the sweet musty smell of hay although it was a little dusty as it was pitched up onto the wagon. Dorothy then drove the wagon to where the rick was to be built and the men unloaded it. Dorothy had driven wooden stakes in the ground to mark the corners of the rick. Noreen and I spread the hay out on the ground with our rakes to the four corner markers, then took a rest until the next load arrived. When we were rested, we rode the wagon out to the field again to collect the next load and help with spreading the hay on the wagon. The hayrick gradually got higher. As we were on top spreading the hay around, we had to be very careful that we didn't get too near the edges and slide off. To get off, we had to climb down a ladder that Dorothy had put up at the opposite end of the rick to where the hay was being loaded. By the end of the afternoon everyone was tired.

The next day was a Sunday and as there was no postal delivery, Len and his friends said they would come back at nine thirty in the morning to help Dorothy to bring in the rest of the hay. She hoped to have it completed on Sunday, in case the weather turned bad in the next few days.

Noreen and I walked back to Post Farm with Dorothy and drove the cows home ahead of us after locating them on the common where they were grazing. Tinker was a big help because he would search out the cows and save us a lot of walking to find the stragglers. He would never bite them but would bark and snap close to their rear legs, sometimes get a kick if he was not quick enough to duck away from an annoyed cow. After they were all in the milking stalls we went in for supper. It was a long day for all of us and tomorrow would be as well. Dorothy's day was not finished as she still had the milking to do before her day was over.

After supper I fed Chuggy and gave him some much-needed water as his trough was completely dry again. Noreen and I then fed the bantams, after which she went into the milking stalls to help her mother, and

Mark Carlile

I retired to the front step to enjoy the evening sun with Tinker and my bird book.

It was another really hot day on Sunday, but Noreen and I did not get up until late after our long day on Saturday. Gran packed a big lunch basket with sandwiches, bottles of water, apples and a flask of coffee for Dorothy and the men. Noreen and I carried it up to the top field at ten thirty. When we arrived at the hayrick, Len and his friends were taking a break, sitting on the ground with their backs against the hayrick, passing around a cider flagon which Uncle Len had filled from his cider barrel before he left home. They put their finger through the hole in the handle by the neck, rested the earthenware flagon against the back of their wrist, tilted it and raised it to their lips and took a drink. After it was passed around, Uncle Len took a final swig before putting the cork in the top. Uncle Len made his own cider every year and had a large wooden barrel of cider in his garden shed. Friends gathered in the shed to partake of the scrumpy after Len completed his postal route in and around Stockland, generally about three thirty depending on the weather. Many years later, Len was featured in a BBC documentary program about West Country life showing the lost art of scrumpy making. He had his own apple orchard and a friend with a cider press, always helped him to make his cider. He only made enough cider for himself and his friends.

In later years, I remember having a glass of cider with him one Christmas in his dirt floor tool shed. I could smell the sour smell of cider as soon as I walked into the dark little shed that had no windows. He said he had a secret in the making of his cider which he did not tell the locals. I asked him what it was.

"I put a little sugar with it. But don't tell anyone."

I promised not to tell.

Noreen and I got up on the empty hay wagon and helped spread the hay as the wagon returned to the field and was re-loaded again. Dorothy brought in several more loads and, at noon, stopped for lunch. The

The Start of Summer

men had brought bread and cheese for lunch but also appreciated some of Gran's sandwiches with their flagon of cider. The hard physical work of haying had given them a good appetite.

We helped until mid-afternoon, until the afternoon break, when we carried the lunch basket back home. As we crossed the common I could hear a curlew calling and saw it fly up a short distance down the hill but my search for its nest revealed nothing. Smart, crafty bird, I thought. Fooled me again.

The cows had been turned out in the field behind the cowshed, so just before supper Noreen and I along with Tinker only had a very short walk to bring them in for Dorothy. When she came home at four thirty, she flopped in a chair and said "I'm glad the haying is finished for another year." And went to sleep.

Gran had a caravan at Sand Bay Caravan Park. The small bay is between Budleigh Salterton and Exmouth, and about forty miles from Post Farm. We had been going to the caravan for a week's holiday for the past few years and really looked forward to going in the sea and playing on the beach. I don't remember when Gran bought the caravan, or how she could afford to keep it there; I only recall the wonderful holidays Noreen and I had there with her. Dorothy could not afford the time off to be with us because she had to do the milking in the mornings and evenings. Cows don't take holidays from giving milk Dorothy would say.

Following the weekend that Dorothy completed the haying, we loaded up the car early on the Saturday morning and after milking Dorothy drove us to Sandy Bay. It took about two hours to make the trip, arriving at the caravan about eleven o'clock. After we had lunch in the caravan, we changed into our swimming costumes, and with our buckets and spades made our way down the steep path from the top of the cliff to the beach. Dorothy stayed with us, relaxing on the hot sunny beach for a few hours until her drive home at four o'clock for milking. She planned to come back on Sunday of the next week to pick us up.

Noreen and I spent most of our time in the water and digging in the sand making sand sculptures. Gran went paddling in the gentle surf. When we returned to the caravan, Gran sat down for a rest after her exhausting climb up the steep path from the beach. We set up a table and chairs on the grass outside the caravan where we planned to eat our meals if it did not rain. When Gran was rested, she heated up our supper of shepherd's pie. This was followed by apple and blackberry pie for dessert, all brought from home. We loved eating outside in the warmth of the evening and listening to the waves gently lapping the shore down at the beach. After supper, we played board games until the sun started to go down. Gran folded up the table and chairs and stored them below the caravan. She asked Noreen and me to fill a pail with water from a tap, a short walk up the gravel road near our caravan, because she needed water for the dishes and washing. After helping with the dishes, we played card games and Monopoly by candlelight until Gran said it was time to go to bed. The caravan had two bunk beds at the front near the kitchen, and the dining table and side seating converted into a double bed where Gran would be sleeping.

"I want to sleep in the top bunk," Noreen said.

"I want to sleep in the top bed," I replied.

"You can take turns," Gran replied. "Noreen tonight and you tomorrow, Michael."

"Alright I suppose." I replied.

Gran made up the beds with our help, and after cleaning our teeth in the sink, we went to bed. It was fun sleeping in a caravan, we talked for a while until Gran told us to go to sleep.

When I awoke in the morning, it was raining. A strong wind was rocking the caravan and heavy rain lashed at the small window near my head. I was disappointed by the rain because we would not be able to go to the beach. The rain on the tin roof of the caravan was comforting as I snuggled down in the warmth under the covers listening to the lashing rain.

After breakfast, it was still raining, so we had to be content with reading books, playing board games and listening to stories from Gran about her childhood, which she loved to relate. The next morning the sky was grey and overcast and it was still raining, but not quite so hard and the wind had settled down to occasional gusts. Another day in the caravan waiting for the weather to clear. Before lunch, Gran sent us up to the small grocery shop at the entrance to the park to get pork chops, sausages and bread. She had brought enough vegetables from home to last the week.

"Put on your raincoats, hats and rubber boots," she reminded us, "or you'll get wet."

"Can we buy an ice cream?" Noreen asked.

"Only a small one," Gran replied, "if they have them."

The rain and wind were in our faces as we made our way up the gravel road of the park to the small shop. We were glad to get inside out of the elements and noticed that they did sell ice cream. After getting the provisions for Gran, we each had a small ice cream cone and stood in the shop eating it. The walk back to the caravan was easier because the wind was at our backs. We were a little wet from our walk, because of the blowing rain, so Gran made us change into dry clothes. There was no heat in the caravan but we used blankets to cover us to keep warm. There was a little heat from the gas stove as Gran made soup for lunch, so that helped. Another afternoon was spent playing cards with Gran and reading until supper was ready.

"I hope it will be sunny tomorrow so that we can go to the beach," Noreen said.

"I expect it will," Gran replied. "The sky looks like it is clearing a little."

It was still raining when we went to bed. I snuggled down under the covers and listened to the rain pattering on the roof as I drifted off to sleep thinking of the beach. The follow morning it had stopped raining, and the sky was starting to clear. By the afternoon the sun was out again but there were still some clouds in the sky. We spent the afternoon on the beach but did not stay in the water very long as the sea was cold. We had four more good days on the beach with lots of sun before Dorothy came back on the Sunday in the late morning to pick us up to return home. The Sunday was really hot so Gran left a note on the caravan door telling Dorothy that we were at the beach. Gran had packed lunch, and we left for the beach early so that we could have all day on the beach for our last day. Dorothy arrived at eleven and quickly changed into her swimming costume and came in the sea with us. After lunch we swam and played in the surf with a rubber car inner tube that Dorothy had brought for us. At three o'clock Gran said it was time to pack up as Dorothy had to get back for milking.

"Just a little longer," I said to Gran.

"Ten minutes, and then we have to go."

As we walked up the steep sandy path from the beach to the park, I turned and said, "Goodbye Sandy Bay, see you next year."

We packed up all our things at the caravan, and Gran tidied up and cleaned the countertops before locking up the caravan for our long trip home. It was a hot trip home in our Rover. Dorothy tilted out the front window so that we could get a little cool air in the car. Very little was said on the trip home from our holiday as we were both sad that the week had ended instead of just beginning, and our summer holidays were coming to an end.

When we got home Tinker rushed up to greet us, wagging his tail with the joy of our return. At least he was glad that we were home again.

Chapter 8

Bloodhounds and Police

It was early September when we returned to school in Honiton after our summer holidays. Returning to school was an indication that summer was coming to an end but we could still get some warm weather. However, the days were drawing in and it would get dark a lot earlier; also we would soon be getting up in the twilight. The first day back at school was always a little unsettling because we would probably have a new teacher and possibly some new kids in our class. Although, it was nice to see all our friends and swap summer stories.

About a week after we returned to school, a small aircraft flew low over our farm and seemed to follow the road up Post Lane and then circled over a neighbour's property just up the road. It was a Saturday morning, and we thought it was someone on a sightseeing trip. It was unusual because we had never seen a small plane fly over our farm before.

We were now riding our bikes to the Rising Sun Farm to catch the school bus. Dorothy had talked to the owners of the farm who said we could put our bikes in a shed while we were at school because we did not want them stolen. When it was raining, Dorothy drove us up to the Rising Sun in the morning because she didn't want us going to school wet. If it was raining when we came back at about four o'clock, Dorothy would pick us up again. If the weather was good we would walk home along the Roman Road, then down Boilen's lane and across the common to Gypsy Manley's cottage.

My eighth birthday in September was fast approaching, and I hoped that Gran would get me the air rifle I so badly wanted. I would have to wait and see.

On Tuesday it was raining hard when we got up to go to school, so Dorothy drove us up to the Rising Sun to catch the bus. She said she would pick us up again at four o'clock because she had to get petrol in the car from Jauncey's garage. It rained on and off all day but when Dorothy picked us up at four it had stopped. We sat in the car while Mr. Jauncey put petrol in the car. Dorothy could only buy a few gallons because petrol was still on ration. When we were driving down Post Lane and had just passed the laneway to Snodwell Farm, we could see several cars and a van on the grassy entrance to a field, right opposite the sharp right-hand bend in the lane. As we approached the vehicles, we could see that there were two police cars, and the back door of the van was open. Several big dogs jumped out of the van and were held on a leash by a policeman. Two more policemen were standing by the cars talking.

"What are those dogs?" I asked.

"Bloodhounds," Dorothy replied.

Dorothy slowed down and stopped as we got to the corner because the narrow lane was blocked by the hounds. She opened her window and asked one of the policemen what was happening.

"Nothing to be concerned about," he replied. "We are just making routine enquiries. No need to worry ma'am. Do you live near here?"

"Yes we do, just down the road at Post Farm. The next farmhouse on the left."

Bloodhounds and Police

"Thank you ma'am, the road is clear now. You may proceed, sorry for delaying you."

While Dorothy was talking to the policeman, Noreen and I were watching the policeman with the bloodhounds. After they had sniffed all around the car, the policeman led them up Post Lane and made a left turn down the narrow overgrown track that went to Bucehayes Cottage. We could see this through the narrow rear window of the car.

"Those hounds went down that track to Bucehayes Cottage," Noreen told Dorothy. "I wonder what could have happened."

"Probably nothing much. The policeman said it was routine enquiries," Dorothy replied.

"Who lives there?" I asked

"Someone called Swann," Dorothy replied. "I have never met or seen him."

When we got home, Gran had supper ready as we walked through the door. Over supper Dorothy told Gran about the bloodhounds and police.

"I expect it will be in the newspaper if it is anything serious," Gran replied.

We didn't think too much more about it and generally we only got the newspaper once a week when Dorothy and Gran shopped for groceries at the village store in Stockland.

Gran said that Aunty Muriel, Uncle Cecil, Gilda and Garry were coming for my birthday which was on Thursday, but they would not be able to come until the Sunday. I was getting excited as I only had one more day to wait.

When we returned from school on Thursday, I rushed into the house to find a birthday cake sitting on the table along with a card, a very small package about the size of a matchbox, a larger package and a very long package, all wrapped up in bright-coloured paper. My heart was pounding as I tore open the wrapping from the long package as Gran watched from the scullery door. I immediately noticed the picture of an air rifle on the box and knew what it was.

"An air rifle!" I exclaimed. "Thank you Gran, thank you."

I rushed up to her and gave her a kiss on the cheek. As I removed the cover from the box and the paper wrapping, there was my air rifle. I took it from the box and carefully examined its dull black and wood surfaces and put it to my shoulder and lined up the sights. It was like a real rifle and I felt comfortable holding it under my arm like I had seen John Sangster do with his twenty-two. I put it down in the box and unwrapped the very small package which was a box of five hundred pellets for my rifle.

"Thanks Gran," I said. "Now I'll be able to shoot rabbits."

I opened the third package which had a note card on the outside that said 'from Dorothy and Noreen'. When I opened the box, I found a pair of brown leather gloves and a brown scarf. I tried on the gloves which had a warm fleece lining and felt warm and comfortable. I wrapped the scarf around my neck and it felt a lot warmer than my old blue scarf which was starting to get ragged.

"Thank you, Noreen. I will be able to use these when we cycle to school and back. They will keep me warm this winter."

Dorothy was out in the yard getting the cows in for milking, and would be in as soon as Gran yelled out the back door that supper was ready. I helped Gran lay the table, putting out the place mats, and knives and forks, and Noreen put out the dinner plates and a small plate for my birthday cake.

"What's for supper, Gran?" I yelled out.

"Shepherd's Pie," came the reply.

"Goody, my favourite!"

Gran made wonderful shepherd's pie with lots of thick gravy. She knew that I really liked it as I always asked for seconds. I took another look at my rifle. Inside

Bloodhounds and Police

the box I found a cardboard target folded up which I would be able to use for practice. I was hoping to go out shooting after we had supper. But as it was getting dark so early, I didn't know if it would be light enough. The rabbits were always out feeding on grass just before dark. I had seen them many times in the lower field as I approached the gate at the bottom of the orchard.

I heard Gran yell out the back door that supper was ready so I sat up in my usual place at the table waiting for Gran to bring in the hot dish of shepherd's pie. It was steaming when Gran brought it in and placed it on a wooden mat on the table. I could hear Dorothy washing her hands in the scullery, and then she came in and sat down at the table.

"Thank you for my gloves and scarf," I said. "They are both nice and warm and will keep me warm when we cycle to school and back."

"Do the gloves fit you? I wasn't sure what size to get."

"Yes, they fit well."

"That's good."

Gran served up the shepherd's pie and reminded us to be careful as it was very hot. After I had eaten my second helping, Gran cleared away the dishes with Noreen's help and then placed my birthday cake in front of me and lit the candles. They sang 'Happy Birthday' to me and then I blew out all the candles. She cut us all a slice and dished it up onto our plates. It was a chocolate cake that had white icing on the outside and chocolate icing in the middle. It also had a few cherries in it. Chocolate cake was both mine and Noreen's favourite. It was really delicious, but I didn't have a second piece because I was really full from the shepherd's pie. I went outside after supper and set up the target in the garden. It was getting really dark, partly due to the overcast sky, so I only had a few practice shots. I hit the target but not in the middle, so I folded up the target and returned to the dining room.

Mark Carlile

On Saturday, Gran and Dorothy went into Stockland in the afternoon to get groceries, and Noreen and I went along. Mrs. Clark told Gran and Dorothy about a missing man that lives down Post Lane at Bucehayes Cottage.

"So that's why the police and bloodhounds were in Post Lane the other day," Gran said. "I wondered what that was all about."

Mrs. Clark said it was in the Saturday Western Morning News.

"I'll have to get a paper at Mrs. Durrent's shop when we leave and read about it," Gran replied.

"It's on the front page," Mrs. Clark said.

Gran got a newspaper from outside Mrs. Durrent's shop while Dorothy continued shopping. She also slipped in to see Nancy briefly, who lived next door to Mrs. Clark's shop. She returned to help Dorothy complete the grocery shopping and pack the groceries into bags and boxes. Noreen and I bought our usual bag of sweets before we left. When we returned to the car, Gran opened the Western Morning News at the front page, as Dorothy started the car, and there it was, with headlines that read:

Man who came to Devon missing, says Yard.

WIFE: I SAW HIM LAST WEEK AT SEATON.

There was also a picture of him in a black evening suit and bow tie. Gran read it out as Dorothy was driving home.

SCOTLAND YARD yesterday issued a description and photograph of a 65-year-old London man for whom the Devon county police have been searching since September, 1947.

The man, Richard Rhodd Swann, of Sharps-Lane Ruislip, Middlesex, left Stockland near Honiton on

Bloodhounds and Police

September 28, 1947, after saying that he was going to walk to Taunton. He was on a visit to his wife, who was staying in Bucehayes Cottage, Stockland, at the time. Bucehayes is in a desolate part of the parish, right off the beaten track.

The chief constable of Devon (Lieut-Col. R.R.M. Bacon) has been unable to find any evidence that Mr. Swann reached Taunton, and he has not returned to his home in Ruislip.

Mrs. Swann, a 37-year-old qualified nurse, who is now living in a furnished bungalow, Westwell, Burrow-road Seaton, Devon, said last night: "I am completely in the dark what it is all about. I saw my husband last Saturday at this house."

"He was looking very much fitter than usual, and he talked about settling money for the children's education."

"He had shaved off his mustache. He always carries an umbrella, and nearly always a little black bag."

'Malevolent gossip'.

Mrs. Swann asserted that the "whole thing" had been started by malevolent gossip. Inquiries seem to have been started at the London end.

She said that in September, 1947, her husband, who was a businessman in London, visited her in Stockland. He left saying he was going to walk to Taunton. Since then, she said, she has seen him once or twice, either at Stockland or at Seaton, where she had been living the past six months.

Mrs. Swann had been interviewed by Divisional Detective Inspector Green, of Scotland Yard, and detectives from Devon County Police.

A Scotland Yard spokesman told a 'Western Morning News' London reporter last night: We were asked by Devon Police to give this case publicity, and we were interested in that this man was reported missing in London at approximately the same time as he was reported missing in Devon.

Mark Carlile

How they met

Earlier last evening, wearing a light blue marocain frock with small dark spots, Mrs. Swann, who brushed her chestnut hair out of her blue eyes as she spoke in a cultured, educated voice, said she was in charge of a nursing home at Winchelsea when she first met Mr. Swann. Mr. Swann's aunt went to the nursing home. When the aunt died she was cremated in accordance with a provision of her will.

Mr. Swann proposed marriage, said Mrs. Swann and settled two thousand pounds on her.

They were married in London in 1938, and on the certificate Mrs. Swann was described as Miss Kathleen Mercer, spinster, 26, and Mr. Swann age 53, was described as a tea merchant.

Mr. Swann had offices at that time in Crutched Friars, in the City, and owned four houses, one at Ruislip called Hazledean, two at Northwood, Pinner, and a lonely house at Stockland.

Mr. and Mrs. Swann separated in 1942, and Mrs. Swann went to live at Stockland with the two sons

'Stories spread'

Mrs. Swann said that people had spread all kinds of stories about her. One was that Mr. Swann kept five thousand pounds worth of jewels in a strong box and that she had helped herself to the valuables since his alleged disappearance.

"Look at me now," she said, surveying the carpet-less floor and broken-down furniture in the front room of her bungalow. "Does it look like I have five thousand pounds?"

Mrs. Swann said that her husband was a terrific walker and used to cover miles of Devon Heath and woodlands, although people had seen him walking with sticks in Ruislip.

Mrs. Swann is receiving the rent of the house at Honiton, and is in need of money to complete the education of her children.

Bloodhounds and Police

Polish airman

Later last night Mrs. Swann, changed into a smart two-piece navy blue costume, and wearing a decorative platinum ring on her marriage finger told a reporter how she met a Polish airman while he was stationed at Northolt and she was living at Ruislip.

"As soon as my husband heard of my friendship with the Polish airman he invited him to tea, saying he was very interested in happenings on the continent and in several continental towns my friend might have visited."

Tall, broad-shouldered, 14-stone Feliks Marek, age 32, said he was now employed as a builder's labourer at Colyton, a neighbouring village.

He said he joined the Polish Air Force in 1936 and was shot down the third day after the war with Germany broke out. He was wounded and was taken to hospital. Gradually the hospitals were forced back by the advancing Germans, but as he limped along on crutches he managed to hook up with his squadron, and eventually they arrived in Romania.

From there they made their way to Syria, and from Syria to France.

The remnants of his squadron were then re-formed in the French Air Force, and he flew light bombers until the fall of France.

He escaped to Britain and joined the Polish squadron of the R.A.F. It was while he was stationed at Northolt that he met Kathleen Swann.

Marek said he was with his squadron at an airfield in Lincolnshire at the time that Mr. Swann was said to have disappeared.

During his flying career, which he started with flying clubs in Poland at the age of 18, he reached the rank of warrant officer.

Police officers have been baffled because Mr. Swann was reticent about himself and his occupation.

Mr. John McGillycuddy a lodger at Mrs. Swann's house in Ruislip, said that all he could gather was that

Mr. Swann carried on a small business selling tea to a few customers in private houses in the district.

Wire signed 'Kathleen'

"On September 27, 1947 — the last time I saw him — he asked me shortly before 8 o'clock in the morning what the time was, and when I told him he said: 'I must be off or I will be late?'

"On the previous Thursday, two days before, he had received a telegram, and although I did not know what was in it — he would never discuss matters like that — I understood he was going down to Seaton to see Mrs. Swann."

"I understood from him that Mrs. Swann had been living down in that part of the world for about five years."

"We were expecting him back on the following Tuesday, but we heard nothing until the Thursday week, when a telegram came for him and we opened it in his absence. It said: 'Are you coming to Exeter on Saturday'? and was signed Kathleen."

"The next day a woman came who said she was Mrs. Swann, she spent three days with us. Since then I have sent her the rent to her address in Westwell, Burrow-road, Seaton."

He understood from Mr. Swann that the house was left him by an aunt, Miss Ida Farran, who also left him jewellery.

Devon enquiries

Mr. Swann is described as 5ft 11in in height, slim build, thin face, pale complexion, fair hair turning grey, blue eyes, and wearing glasses. He may have a mustache, walks with a pronounced stoop, and uses a stick or umbrella.

So far as Scotland Yard inquiries at Ruislip under Det.-Inspr. Green can discover, Mr. Swann never returned to his home after his visit to Stockland in 1947.

He was reported to the local police as missing in October 1947, and the Devon police are trying to find out whether he is living in any other part of Devon.

Bloodhounds and Police

They do not believe he is suffering from loss of memory, and there do not appear to be any circumstances which might cause him to live under an assumed name.

Noreen and I were listening as Gran read the article. "Do you think he was murdered?" I asked.

"Well, it is very strange," Gran said. "The police obviously think something happened at that cottage or they wouldn't have had bloodhounds there the other day. I am sure we will hear more about it in the coming days."

When we arrived home, I decided to see if there were any rabbits in the lower field. I got my rifle from the corner of the dining room where I had it standing, and the pellets from the window seat, and walked down the garden to the gate by the outhouse and into the orchard. The orchard had a sweet smell of apples as they ripened on the trees. Some had already fallen and were being attacked by wasps. I always gave them a light kick to roll them over before picking one up off the grass in case a wasp had burrowed into the underside. Some of the dropped apples that were bruised were starting to rot and were baking in the sunlight giving off a distinctive musky smell.

It was a beautiful sunny afternoon, perhaps a little early to see rabbits but possibly they would be out sunning themselves. I had already put a pellet in my rifle and approached the gate to the lower field very slowly and quietly, and from the far left so that a rabbit would not see me. As I moved to the gate, I could only see two rabbits that were quite far away but I decided to take a shot at one of them. I gently rested my rifle on the top of the gate and aligned the sights with the nearest rabbit. He had heard something because his ears were up. I slowly squeezed the trigger and after the bang both rabbits ran for their holes in the hedge.

Mark Carlile

I will have to come back later, I thought, when more rabbits would be out eating.

I returned home feeling a little dejected, but after all, this was my first try so I'll keep trying.

I went into Post Lane and loaded my rifle again and took some shots at birds sitting in the trees. I hit a thrush, and it dropped through the tree to the ground, dead.

I returned my rifle to the dining room along with the pellets.

Over supper that evening, Gran reminded me that Aunty Muriel, Uncle Cecil, and the children were coming on Sunday for my birthday, and that we had to have a bath tonight so that we can put on clean clothes for Sunday. She told me not to wander off tomorrow which Noreen and I often did. Sometimes we would be gone all morning or afternoon, and I would come back filthy dirty if I had been climbing trees.

On Sunday morning Gran gave us both clean clothes and said, "Don't get dirty, you two."

Aunty Muriel's car arrived outside the garden gate just before one o'clock. We all went out to greet them, and Gran said to come in as she had lunch ready.

We hadn't seen them for a long time. I think it was last Christmas when we had dinner with them at Holmead Farm.

Aunty Muriel gave me a small package and said "Happy birthday, Michael." I quickly tore off the wrapping and found a tool bag for my bicycle.

"Thank you, Aunty Muriel and Uncle Cecil," I said, "that's just what I wanted."

Gran had cooked a roast of pork, and had apple sauce, brussel's sprouts, roast potatoes, carrots, Yorkshire pudding and gravy. Gran knew this was also one of my favorite dinners. She knew exactly what I liked.

Gary was four years old and Gilda three, and they sat each side of their mother on one side of the table so that she could help them.

Bloodhounds and Police

"You have done us proud, Mother," Muriel said. "This is an excellent dinner, we did not expect you to cook all this."

Cecil said very little, except when he was asked a question which was normal for him. He was a man of few words but a very nice person.

Gran had made an apple and blackberry pie and custard for dessert with clotted cream. She had been busy cooking all morning from the time we got up.

Noreen and I played with Garry and Gilda in the living room after dinner, reading stories and playing Snakes and Ladders, until Muriel said it was time to go as Uncle Cecil had to get back for milking. He had a large farm near Tiverton with about twenty-five milking cows. We said goodbye to them at the garden gate as they left and waved as their little car drove down Post Lane.

I got my little tool bag and strapped it to my bicycle saddle with the two leather straps provided. It was small, so would only carry a few spanners which I would have to get later. Perhaps for Christmas.

Mark Carlile

Chapter 9

Where is Richard Swann?

The following week when we cycled up Post Lane on the Monday to catch the bus at the Rising Sun, we noticed a policeman standing at the entrance to the laneway of Bucehayes Cottage. He was also there when we returned from school in the evening. Noreen mentioned it to Gran, and she said that Dorothy had also seen him when she took the milk to the top of the lane for the milk truck, and when she collected the empty churns later on.

On Tuesday it was raining again when we got up to go to school so Dorothy drove us up to the Rising Sun to catch the school bus. We took shelter in the shed where we normally kept our bicycles until the bus came, and as soon as we heard it stop we dashed out and jumped on.

It rained all day so we couldn't go outside at lunchtime and had to be content with staying in the large lunchroom for our lunch break. None of us enjoyed that.

It had stopped raining when the school bus returned us to the Rising Sun, therefore we had to walk home again along the Roman road and down Boilen's lane, which was very muddy from all the rain. We tried to keep to the grass verge where it was not quite so wet to keep our shoes from getting clogged with mud. When we climbed over the gate at the end of the lane, we cleaned our shoes in the long grass to get some of the mud off. As we went down the track across the common, I noticed a number of cars and motorbikes at the back of Bucehayes Cottage, and lots of people milling around. Some were policemen and others appeared to be wearing white clothing. This was the only spot where Bucehayes Cottage can be seen because it is in a very secluded spot, surrounded by hills, trees and common.

We hurried down the track in case someone was lurking behind the high gorse bushes ready to jump on us. It appeared that someone had been murdered there, otherwise there would not be all those policemen and bloodhounds.

We were soon crossing Gypsy Manley's yard and making our way down Post Lane.

"Take those muddy shoes off," Gran said as we came in the front door. "Why did you come down Boilen's lane and across the common instead of keeping to the road after all this rain today? You must have known it would be muddy?"

"It was quicker," I replied.

"You two better clean your shoes after supper. I have enough to do without that."

"Yes Gran," I said.

We ate supper in silence but after supper I told Gran and Dorothy about all the cars, motorcycles and police at Bucehayes Cottage.

"Something serious must have happened at that Cottage," Gran said to Dorothy, "for all those vehicles to be there."

"Nancy said she takes the Western Morning News every day. She said she will keep it for us. We will be able to read the articles when I get them from Nancy on Saturday after we go to Stockland."

When we returned from grocery shopping the following Saturday, Gran had collected several

Where is Richard Swann?

newspapers from Aunty Nancy. From Monday to Saturday there were articles about the missing Mr. Swann. Monday's paper had another long article. "At least we can use all these newspapers for toilet paper," Gran said. After we ate supper, Gran cleared away the supper dishes and washed them with Noreen and me helping to wipe. She made a pot of tea and sat in her armchair with a cup of tea and read the article in the Monday paper about Mr. Swann. It included several pictures of Bucehayes Cottage, one of the furnished bungalow in Seaton where Mrs. Swann now resides, and one of Mrs. Swann.

Monday's headlines read:

Devon C.I.D. has no news of Mr. Swann

WIFE TELLS OF HIS VISITS TO HER IN SEATON

Devon C.I.D. officers, directed by Det.-Supt W.C. Harvey, were yesterday checking the numerous reports that had come in from the public in response to the nation-wide search for Richard Rhodd Swann, the 64-year-old London tea merchant.

Supt. Harvey told the 'Western Morning News' that since Mr. Swann's picture and description were issued by Scotland Yard on Friday no-one has come forward with any definite information regarding his whereabouts, except his 37-year-old wife, Mrs. Kathleen Swann.

Supt. Harvey added: "We want to find him in order to close our files on this case." He indicated that the search for Mr. Swann would go on for several days before a definite line of action was taken.

On September 28, 1947, Mr. Swann, of Sharps-Lane, Ruislip, Middlesex, left Stockland, near Honiton, after visiting his wife, who then lived at Bucehayes Cottage, saying he was going to walk to Taunton. The police have been unable to find anyone except Mrs. Swann who has seen him since.

Mrs. Swann, who now lives in a furnished bungalow, Westwell, Burrow-road, Seaton, Devon, sat up talking until 1:30 yesterday morning to a 'Western Morning News' reporter. She told how, on February 16 of this year, her husband, whom she thought was dead, made a dramatic appearance in the evening.

While Mrs. Swann spoke of her life with Mr. Swann, Feliks Marek, the 32-year-old Polish ex-warrant officer pilot, who is her friend made innumerable cups of tea. Mrs. Swann said: "I have hardly slept at all since the police came here on Tuesday."

It was because she was anxious to get the matter cleared up that Mrs. Swann and Mr. Marek sat up talking for nearly four hours on Saturday night and yesterday morning.

'Worth 15,000 pounds'

Mrs. Swann said at the beginning of the war her husband told her he was worth 15,000 pounds. In the early part of 1947 he said that if she would go back to him (they were separated at the time) she would have her own house, and have her own car, and would give the boys a good education.

"I left him in May 1942," said Mrs. Swann, "and he disappeared from Stockland in September, 1947. I thought he was dead until February 16, last, when he turned up here at Seaton. 'I said to him: why didn't you keep away. I thought you were dead. Why didn't you stay dead'?"

Mrs. Swann said that her husband arrived at about 9 o'clock in the evening and left the house about 11 p.m. He next turned up on March 5.

She had reached Seaton from Exeter by train at about 9 p.m., and when she walked out of the station her husband was standing on the corner of Borrow-road.

Where is Richard Swann?

"I started a campaign of asking for money from him," she continued, *"in order to obtain a good school education for the boys."*

'Kept visiting us'

"He kept visiting us. He came seven or eight time at intervals of three to six days. The last time I saw him was last Saturday. He just came to the house and knocked on the door.

"First he said he was living on a fishing boat, then I gather he was living in a sort of monastery.

"He always used to be badly dressed, but he now surprised me, as he was quite smart. He was wearing a white shirt and black suit. He always used to wear a bowler, but now he was wearing a black Homburg. In fact, he was smartly done up. He looked better, healthier, and weathered in every way than before he disappeared.

"When he came last week, he said he was coming back this week, If he had come back I was going to get Felix to hold him for the police, but he won't arrive now because of all this publicity. My husband never left any address, but I always found he was living nearby in this district."

Go out for a drink

Mrs. Swann added: *"I would never go back to my husband under any conditions. As far as he was concerned, however, there was never a definite break between us.*

"What happened was that the children had had pneumonia and I went down to Stockland with them. I used to go up to see him, but these visits decreased. The last time I went up to visit him, was in March, 1947."

On Friday and Saturday evening Mrs. Swann and Felix Marek went out to a local hotel for a drink.

"We do not often do this" said Marek, who works as a builder's labourer, *"for we cannot afford it, but now with this trouble it makes a break."*

Mark Carlile

Asked if he were ever going back to Poland, he emphatically replied. "No. Those of us who have been in the West are marked with the beast, as it were."

Over the weekend police kept a constant watch on Bucehayes Cottage. Yesterday afternoon its whitewashed walls partly covered with creepers, the cottage stood out brightly in the spring sunshine. A curlew piped overhead and chickens pecked all around.

The cottage which has three bedrooms, its own electricity power plant, and a telephone, is at present tenanted by Mr. L.V. Hall and his wife and family.

Mr. Hall said he visited Mrs. Swann at the cottage once before taking over tenancy last October, but the negotiations were conducted through a solicitor. He sent the rent, which was over one pound a week, to Mrs. Swann once a quarter.

When Mr. Swann set out to walk to Taunton, from the cottage in September 1947, his quickest route would have been to strike straight across Bucehayes common, and to follow the public footpath which would lead him onto the old Roman road. The whole route lies across sparsely populated countryside.

On Saturday afternoon, Mrs. Swann went to Seaton railway station, where she asked the station-master if he had seen her husband recently.

The station master had no recollection of seeing Mr. Swann, although he was shown a photograph that appeared in Saturday's 'Western Morning News'.

Earlier, Mrs. Swann had said: "Stanley and the mad parson and 25,000 deserters are missing and cannot be found, so why it is so unusual that my husband has disappeared and cannot be found?"

Gran sat the paper down and had another cup of tea.

When Dorothy came in from milking, Gran made her some fresh tea and she sat down with the tea and biscuits with her feet up, also reading the article.

Where is Richard Swann?

When she had finished reading, she discussed it with Gran.

"If Mr. Swann had visited Mrs. Swann at Seaton seven or eight times, knowing the police could not find him, why didn't Mrs. Swann contact the police and tell them he was at her house? It doesn't make sense. Also, the only time she and her Polish boyfriend decided to hold him, he doesn't show up."

"She said she needed money from Mr. Swann for the boys' education but she seemed to have no idea where he was living, or mentioned anything about him giving her money. Also, she was renting Bucehayes Cottage when it belonged to Mr. Swann. If she thought he was living locally why did she go to the Seaton station-master to see if he had seen Mr. Swann?"

"I had the same thoughts," Gran said. "I think Mrs. Swann and her Polish boyfriend murdered Mr. Swann for his money and property. He is probably buried somewhere around that property."

"I wonder where her two boys are going to school," Dorothy said. "I have never seen them around here. They must be going to a private school somewhere. For that matter, I have never seen Mr. or Mrs. Swann either. It is about a fifteen mile walk to Taunton that's a long way to walk. I doubt if he did that."

Noreen and I were listening to this, and Noreen said "Do you think there is still a murderer around, do we need to be careful?"

"No, no," Dorothy replied. "You don't need to be afraid. The Swann's don't live there anymore. Someone is renting Bucehayes Cottage now, and this happened in September 1947."

When we cycled to school in the morning, we decided not to go down across Bucehayes Common on the way home from school for a while. It was generally muddy and wet with puddles down Boilen's Lane, due to all the rain, and the path across the common was also muddy. It was a longer way around on the road if we were not cycling, but it was safer. At least it was not muddy on the road so Gran would be happy.

The policeman was still at the entrance to the lane into Bucehayes Cottage and said hello as we cycled past in the morning. I noticed he was still there when we returned from school. I was going really fast from the momentum I gained down the steep hill just before Snodwell Lane so he did not get a chance to say hello as I flashed past. I liked going down that hill as I could get lots of speed that would take me all the way to the sharp right-hand bend in the lane where the police unloaded the bloodhounds. It was hard work cycling up that hill first thing in the morning, and sometimes we would get off and push when we were halfway up as it was really steep.

Getting home was much quicker now that we had our bicycles, and I had a little time before supper was ready at five. When we returned home that evening, I got my air rifle and pellets and went down the garden to the orchard gate and across the orchard to the lower field. I snuck up on the lower field gate very carefully but there were no rabbits in sight. I would have to come back after supper just before dark. There was a rusty tin can in the field so I took a shot at it and heard the pellet 'click' into it. My sighting was okay I thought.

The apples on the trees were getting really ripe, and I thought that Dorothy would be picking them soon which we always helped with. Uncle Len sometimes came up to help as well. I liked seeing Uncle Len. He was soft-spoken, with a red face, and very strong from delivering the parcels and letters to the farms around Stockland, and he was always willing to help anyone. At Christmas time, he got lots of Christmas tips from the farms he visited as they all knew him. Aunty Nancy was glad to see him home on Christmas Day from his deliveries because people often offered him a Christmas drink on his rounds. He would come back drunk as he did not like to refuse a drink. Aunty Nancy was afraid he would fall off his bicycle and hurt himself.

Where is Richard Swann?

There were lots of dropped and rotting apples in the grass below the trees, which I often kicked like a football. It was good practice.

Gran had supper ready when I got back. She had made bangers and mash with lots of gravy and cabbage. Another one of my favourite meals. Noreen liked it as well. I went back for seconds but was not the last to finish.

"I don't know where you put it all," Gran said. "You need to eat slower or you will get indigestion."

She was always telling me that but I didn't change. After I finished my dessert of baked apple and custard, I rushed out with my air rifle and went down to the lower field to see if the rabbits were out feeding. There were a few but not too close to the gate. I carefully sighted in the nearest one and held my breath and squeezed the trigger. The rabbit leapt into the air sideways and I thought I got him, but he turned and ran back into his hole in the hedge. I jumped over the gate and ran to where I thought his hole was but couldn't find anything. I was very disappointed, and realized that unless I could get nearer to them, my air rifle was just not powerful enough to kill a rabbit. It was starting to get dark, so I walked home thinking that perhaps my air rifle would bring down a pigeon or crow. I would have to try on the weekend.

When I got back, Gran was sitting in her armchair with a cup of tea reading the Tuesday Western Morning News article about Mr. Swann. I looked over her shoulder to read the headlines.

Detectives visit cottage in search for Swann
Missing man's wife said she is leaving Devon soon

In their search for Richard Rhodd Swann, the 64-year-old city merchant, detectives yesterday visited Bucehayes Cottage, Stockland, near Honiton, which Mr.

Mark Carlile

Swann left in September, 1947, after visiting his wife and family, saying he was going to walk to Taunton.

The detectives spent some time in one of the chicken houses, about a dozen of which are situated near the cottage. A new, intensified search of the surrounding countryside is planned by Scotland Yard and Devon police.

Mr. and Mrs. L.V. Hall, Mrs. Swann's tenant at Bucehayes Cottage, said there had been some sightseers during the day.

Divisional Det.-Inspr, W. Green of Wembley, who visited Seaton, Devon, last Tuesday, and interviewed Mrs. Kathleen Swann, Mr. Swann's 37-year-old wife, will travel down again tomorrow.

Mrs. Swann will shortly leave Westwell, Burrowroad, Seaton, where she has been living since she left Bucehayes Cottage, and go back to Hazledean, Sharps-Lane, Ruislip, a house owned by her husband.

Feliks Marek, the 32-year-old Polish ex-pilot who is at present living at her Seaton Bungalow, will go with her.

Telling this to a 'Western Morning News' Reporter yesterday, Mrs. Swann added: "I am going there because the house is owned by my husband, and I am still his wife. I shall take Feliks with me."

Yesterday afternoon Mrs. Swann and Marek went out into the country "to get away from it all." Mrs. Swann said: "We could not go onto the beach very well as everyone would be staring at us."

When Mrs. Swann returned from her trip in the evening she looked sunburnt and well.

600 Pounds in securities

Last night Supt. W.C. Harvey, told the 'Western Morning News' that the police were following routine inquiries in an endeavour to locate Mr. Swann, but so far without success.

"At the moment," he said, "there is nothing doing, nothing to report at all."

Where is Richard Swann?

Mrs. Swann said last night that she has contacted a solicitor to watch her interests as she was naturally having a worrying time.

She also said that on one of his visits sometime in March, her husband had made over to her 600 pounds in securities, mainly industrial.

The suggestion that his signature was a forgery was quite ridiculous, as he had signed the documents in her presence, and Feliks Marek had signed them as a witness.

Mrs. Swann added that when the police visited her last Tuesday they took away with them a stock-brokers list of the securities concerned.

'Never returned'

During the past week three letters, all bearing London postmarks, have arrived for Mr. Swann at his Ruislip house.

The letters are being kept unopened by Mr. John McGillycuddy, who occupies the ground-floor at the house.

Mr. McGillycuddy said yesterday that since Mr. Swann disappeared they had forwarded all his letters to Mrs. Swann in Devon.

"We had known Mr. Swann about six years, and had lived with him in this house for two years. He used to go to London about three days a week on business, but he never went away for any length of time without saying where he was going.

"Frequently he would go to Devon to see his children. In September, 1947, he told us he had received a telegram to go and visit the children and that he would be back about three days later. He never returned.

"After he had been missing about two weeks the police came and forced their way into his room, but could find no clue."

When Gran finished reading I noticed her head drop, and she fell asleep with the newspaper on her lap.

Mark Carlile

To amuse ourselves in the evening, we would often play Monopoly on the floor. Dorothy had a Mahjong set that her ex-husband brought back during the war years. It consisted of 144 tiles with Chinese characters and symbols and is a game of skill and strategy. We didn't know how to play it but used the yellow tiles to build little houses and roads. We kept ourselves amused for hours with the two games, as well as a game of dominoes, which Gran sometimes played with us.

Dorothy came in at eight after finishing the milking and cleaning out the stalls. She had to keep everything very clean to avoid contaminating the milk, and risk rejection by the Milk Marketing Board.

Gran made her usual cup of tea along with a couple of biscuits, and she settled down in the armchair to read the article about Richard Swann. After she had finished reading it, she read through the rest of the paper as Gran did her knitting in the other chair by the fireplace.

"We will soon have to light the fire," Gran said. "It is getting cool in here in the evenings."

"Yes it is," Dorothy replied. "I will get some logs split tomorrow and get them in for you."

"I read the article you just read about Swann," Gran said, "and it now looks like they are starting to look at something in one of the chicken houses for some reason. Also, it looks like Mrs. Swann may have forged Mr. Swann's signature to transfer securities into her name. Conveniently witnessed by that Polish boyfriend. Strange how they are the only two people to have seen Mr. Swann, when the police and all of England can't find him."

"Yes, it is strange," Dorothy replied. "Something really funny going on there."

"You two better get to bed; you have to get up early to go to school in the morning. And pack those games up before you go."

"Aww, do we really have to?" I asked.

"Yes, it's late."

Where is Richard Swann?

We packed the games away, went for our nightly trip to the bottom of the garden, and after cleaning our teeth went to bed.

In the morning when we got up it was raining again. I could smell something nice cooking when I was washing my face before breakfast. The water Gran had put in the basin was hot and felt good as I wiped the sleep from my eyes with a flannel.

Gran had cooked scrambled eggs and bubble and squeak for breakfast as she had some leftover vegetables and potatoes. One of my favourite breakfasts. When we were ready for school, it was raining even harder so we put on our macs and Dorothy got out the car and drove us up to the Rising Sun.

Our teacher had a field trip organized that day as he was going to teach us about vegetables and how to plant and grow them. If the rain did not stop it would have to be cancelled for another day. It was planned for ten o'clock but it looked far too wet at ten. Everyone was really disappointed. Instead, he had a reading class to replace it which I was never fond of. He had each of us come up in front of the class and read a passage from 'Black Beauty' a story about a horse. I always struggled with reading and Gran sometimes made me read to her in the evenings to help me with it. My spelling was bad as well. Noreen never really had any problems with reading or spelling.

When we returned to the Rising Sun, the roads were very wet, but it had stopped raining. We decided that we better walk home as it was doubtful that Dorothy would come to pick us up. It was a long walk back by the roadway and it seemed to take a long time to get to Post Lane. When we passed the laneway to Bucehayes Cottage, a policeman was standing at the entrance and said 'hello' to us as we passed by.

It was almost five o'clock by the time we got in and we both flopped in the armchairs beside the fire for a rest. Gran had a nice roaring fire going in the hearth. She must have recently lit it because the logs were not

Mark Carlile

burnt very much and were spitting and crackling as the flames leapt around them.

"How was school?" Gran asked, as she set the table for supper.

I told her about our cancelled field trip and the reading lesson that we had instead.

"You can read to me later on," she said. "You need lots of practice because your reading needs improvement."

I pretended not to hear, but I knew Gran would be getting my book out later on. She would not forget.

We had vegetable and chicken stew for supper, and apple pie and custard for dessert. I liked pie and always went back for seconds if Gran had made a pie.

I listened to Dick Barton on the radio after Dorothy and Gran had listened to the six o'clock news. It was very faint though possibly due to the bad weather, or perhaps the radio batteries were getting low. I tried adjusting the aerial, but it made no difference.

We helped Gran with the dishes. She said that if the weather was good on the weekend, Dorothy was planning on picking apples so would need our help.

"That will be fun," Noreen replied.

When Gran finished the dishes, she got out 'Treasure Island', the book I was reading with her. We sat by the fire, side by side, as I struggled to read to her.

"Sound the words out," she said to me when I came to a word I could not pronounce. There were many. I was always glad when we were finished as I had very little interest in reading. Pictures were good enough for me.

Gran made her usual pot of tea and sat in her armchair and picked up the Wednesday Western Morning News and read the next article about the Swann disappearance.

The story still had the front page, and Wednesday's headlines read:

Where is Richard Swann?

SWANN MANAGED AUNT'S BUSINESS AFFAIRS

Former servant speaks of his visits to Devon cottage

Mr. Richard Rhodd Swann, the 64-year-old city merchant, for whom Scotland Yard launched a nation-wide publicity campaign, had complete control of the business affairs of Miss Ida Farran, the aunt who left him lonely Bucehayes Cottage, Stockland, near Honiton, from which he set out on September, 1947, to walk to Taunton.

Mrs. Edie Gollop, the wife of Mr. George Gollop, of Percey Farm, Dunkeswell, near Honiton, yesterday told a 'Western Morning News' reporter that Swann was a great favourite of Miss Ida Farran who died at Bucehayes Cottage, on May, 14, 1941.

Mrs. Gollop was a maid and friend of Miss Farran. She went to the cottage 15 years ago during the lifetime of Miss Gertrude Farran, who died in 1935. The Misses Ida and Gertrude Farran were sisters. Miss Gertrude left the cottage to her sister.

Miss Gertrude Farran was not friendly towards Mr. Swann and he seldom visited the cottage during her lifetime. When, however, Miss Ida Farran went from Ruislip to live at Stockland on her sister's death Mr. Swann made frequent visits.

He generally arrived on a Friday and stayed until Sunday, said Mrs. Gollop. Miss Ida Farran's car was sent to pick him up.

"He seldom went out very far," said Mrs. Gollop, "except to walk down the lane. He spent most of his time sitting with Miss Ida Farran and talking to her. He always looked after her business interests."

Talked of shares

Mrs. Gollop, a native of Stockland, was married in 1938. Her husband comes from Lyme Regis. Miss Ida

Mark Carlile

Farran thought so much of Mrs. Gollop's services that, in order that she could stay on and work for her, she allowed Mr. Gollop, who was employed in the district at the time, to live at Bucehayes Cottage also.

During this period Mr. Gollop would sometimes drive Mr. Swann to and from the station on his visits, and he said that Mr. Swann often talked about his share dealings.

On one occasion, in the early part of the war, Mr. Swann rang up from Taunton at 2 a.m. and asked to be picked up.

Mrs. Swann only came down to the cottage on one of these visits.

In March, 1941, Mr. Gollop took over the tenancy of Bethlehem Farm, Offwell, near Honiton, and he and his wife left the cottage.

Bog near cottage

Shortly before the war Miss Ida Farran had a stroke and went into hospital. When she returned to the cottage she was much weaker physically and used a Bath chair. On Mr. and Mrs. Gollop's departure, Mr. Swann went to live at the cottage and looked after Miss Farran until she died a few months later.

In spite of her long service to Miss Farran, Mrs. Gollop was left nothing in her will.

Mrs. Gollop said that Mr. Swann was very quiet and reserved and never brought any friends with him on his visits to Stockland.

There was a bog said Mr. Gollop, between the cottage and the main road. "I once sank into it up to my waist," he added.

Mr. Swann was fit and healthy for his age, in Mr. Gollop's opinion.

Three weeks ago Mr. and Mrs. Gollop moved into their new 70-acre farm at Denkeswell.

Devon C.I.D. reported no developments in the search for Mr. Swann.

Divisional-Det.-Inspr. W. Green, of Wembley, is expected very shortly.

Where is Richard Swann?

Solicitor instructed

Mr. E. Jauncey garage proprietor, of Stockland, told a 'Western Morning News' reporter that when he look Mr. Swann out to Bucehayes Cottage on September 27, 1947, he was dressed in a nondescript manner.

Mrs. Swann had telephoned and asked him to meet Mr. Swann on his arrival at Axminster from London on the late train.

"I have not seen him since," said Mr. Jauncey.

Mrs. Swann also said that the London solicitor who was watching her interests had been instructed to act for Feliks Marek her Polish friend as well.

She refuted reports that she was sending her children away from Seaton to London immediately.

The family would stay together, she said.

Mrs. J. Ford, a former matron of a Seaton nursing home who knew Mr. Swann very well before the war, has stated that she remembers him bringing his aunt and a niece to the nursing home.

No clues

Inquiries made in London yesterday by Divisional Det.-Inspr. Green did not carry the investigation much further.

Mr. Pelham B. Swann, a cousin of Mr. Richard Swann was seen, but was unable to assist the enquiries to any extent, as he had not been in touch with the missing man for about 18 months before his actual disappearance.

Further enquiries are being made in London regarding Mr. Richard Swann's business dealings in the hope that through these channels something might emerge to provide a clue concerning his activities in the closing stages of 1947.

Early yesterday the Devon police investigated the reported find of a walking-stick, umbrella, and a set of dentures in the vicinity of the cottage at Stockland, but it was learned later that they thought the articles were without significance.

Mark Carlile

Gran got out her knitting and continued to knit the pair of grey socks she started a few days ago and did not have time to continue. Noreen and I got out a puzzle and scattered the pieces on a large wooden board that we kept for making puzzles. If we made it on the table, we had to finish it in the same evening as it would have to be packed away before bedtime. This puzzle was large and complicated with lots of small pieces. Gran liked doing puzzles, and if we got stuck would often help out. The picture on the box looked like Switzerland. There were mountains in the background and a log house with two people dressed in brightly coloured clothing walking down a path across a meadow covered in a profusion of wildflowers. We spent the evening pouring over the pieces and only had the outside finished and a little of the mountains before Gran said it was nearly time to go to bed.

Dorothy didn't come in until nine o'clock as she had lots of cleaning to do after milking. Gran had already made her tea as she had expected her in earlier.

"I read the Wednesday article about the Swann's," Gran said to Dorothy. "It said his aunt left him Bucehayes Cottage, and that he handled her business affairs. It talked about the previous ownership of the cottage, and the services of a Mrs. Gollop who worked for the aunt. Not much else of interest if you don't feel like reading it."

"Don't think I will," Dorothy said. "I am really tired tonight."

"Oh, one other thing. They said Mr. Jauncey picked up Swann from Axminster station and took him to Bucehayes Cottage on the weekend he disappeared. They said Mr. Jauncey had a garage in Stockland, which is not correct. It is at the junction of the Roman road and the A30."

"Newspapers get things wrong sometimes, Mum."

Where is Richard Swann?

Noreen and I carried the board that our puzzle was on into the sitting room and carefully put it on the floor by the piano. Then after our trip to the bottom of the garden, we went to bed.

I lay in bed listening to the wind blowing in the trees and occasionally rattling the loose pane of glass in my bedroom window. It was not raining, so perhaps we could cycle up to the Rising Sun to catch the bus in the morning. It was so much quicker than walking, and we didn't have to leave so early. I started thinking about my air rifle and what I could shoot with it. I think I will try pigeons and magpies, I thought, lots of magpies around. Dorothy caught me shooting sparrows in the lane the other day and said I was a cruel little boy. Perhaps I was, and maybe I better not shoot any more of them I thought. The candle in the candlestick was flickering and casting strange shadows around the room for the imagination to ponder. Then it suddenly went out and plunged my bedroom into darkness. It must be the end of the candle I thought. As my thoughts wandered, I slowly drifted off to sleep.

It was not raining in the morning so we used our bicycles to ride up the lane to catch the school bus. The wind was still blowing which helped us once we got onto the Roman road. We put our bikes in the shed at the Rising Sun and joined the other kids waiting for the bus. When the bus stopped at Monkton to pick up more kids, Sally, who was in my class, got on and came to sit beside me. She was tall and thin and always had a spotty face. She smiled and said she was talking to my girlfriend yesterday.

"Who is that?" I asked.

"Wendy Banbury," she said. "You know you like her, I saw you smiling at her in class. She likes you, she told me so."

I didn't say anything, but I did like Wendy. She had long blond wavy hair and a really cute face. I liked her from the first time I saw her.

Mark Carlile

We had maths, English and reading classes for most of the day which I did not enjoy. But later in the afternoon we had the classes I liked — history and geography. When the bell rang, signalling it was time to go home, I quickly put my books and pencils in the desk and rushed out to catch the bus home.

As we cycled past the driveway to Bucehayes Cottage, I noticed that there was still a policeman standing there. We were getting used to seeing him, but it was not always the same policeman. I waved as I flashed by.

When we got home, I got out my air rifle and went down the garden looking for magpies. My bird book said that most people don't like them because they eat other bird's eggs and their young. They are also arrogant and challenging. I walked down the long garden very slowly but did not see any. Then I went out the garden gate and into the orchard and walked around the apple trees but could not see a single magpie. On the weekend I thought I would go into the woods and look for them, pigeons as well. There was not enough time to do that now as Gran would have supper ready at five. I walked back home and put my air rifle away until the weekend.

When we sat down to supper, Dorothy said she would have to get rid of our pig, Chuggy.

"Why?" Noreen asked. "What are you going to do with him?"

"He's got a deep hole in his shoulder, it is about the size of my finger. If we leave it and it gets infected, we may not get any bacon or roasts from him. I have arranged to take him in to have him slaughtered on Friday."

"Oh no," Noreen said. "You can't kill him, he's our pet."

"He was never meant to be a pet, Noreen," her mother replied. "I bought and raised him for the pork meat. I always intended to slaughter him one day; I told you that when I got him, I'm sorry. Perhaps we'll get another baby pig next year if Mrs. Richard has any."

Where is Richard Swann?

There were tears in Noreen's eyes as she ate her supper.

"I'm not eating him," she said, "so don't give me any of him, Gran."

"Alright," Gran replied, knowing that in a few days Noreen will have forgotten all about it.

Noreen was very kind-hearted when it came to animals and would never mistreat or harm an animal. Noreen ate the rest of her supper in silence obviously thinking about Chuggy and his demise.

After supper, we carried out the board with the puzzle on it from by the piano in the sitting room and put it on the table. Noreen sat on one side of the table and I knelt on a chair on the other side. We pored over the giant puzzle. It was a challenge but very slowly we were able to add pieces and it started to look a bit like the picture on the box. Gran came to help for a little while. She loved puzzles, and she found some of the pieces for the meadow with the wildflowers. They fitted at the bottom and were some of the hardest pieces to fit together.

She did not stay long before going into the scullery to make a pot of tea. She sat down in her armchair and rummaged through the pile of newspapers beside her chair until she found Thursday's Western Morning News, and the article about the missing Mr. Swann.

The front page depicted a picture of Mrs. Swann and her solicitor in a car as they left Honiton police station.

The headlines read:

MRS. SWANN VISITS POLICE IN HONITON

Gives 'new information' about husband in two-hour talk

Mrs. Kathleen Swann, wife of Richard Rhodd Swann, for whom a nation-wide search is being conducted, visited

Mark Carlile

Honiton Police Station yesterday afternoon and gave the police new and additional information regarding her husband and his relatives.

Her London solicitor, Mr. Ambrose Appelbe, accompanied her, and afterwards told a 'Western Morning News' reporter: "Mrs. Swann made a long statement to the police which will open up a wide field of enquiries.

"She gave information concerning the death of Richard Swann's aunts in 1937 and 1941. Fresh information which she has given to the police may have an important bearing on his disappearance."

The results of the London enquiries into the disappearance of Mr. Swann will be reviewed at a conference to be held at Scotland Yard today, when Det.-Inspr. Green, who has been in charge of the London investigation, and Det.-Sergt. Phillips, who has been assisting him will confer with the senior officers of the C.I.D.

It is understood they will generally discuss all angles of the inquiries which they have made on behalf of the Devon police in London, and decide what further action they can take.

Buried at Stockland

Mrs. Swann said that the aunts she told the police about were Mrs. Maria Clarkson Swann, who died on February 16, 1937, at Hazledean, Ruislip, and was cremated: and Miss Ida Farran, who died at Bucehayes Cottage, Stockland, on May 14, 1941, and is buried in the parish churchyard at Stockland.

Miss Ida Farran is buried in the same grave as her sister, Miss Gertrude Farran, who died in 1935. Miss Gertrude's name is on the tombstone, but Miss Ida's is not.

Mrs. Swann arrived at Honiton Police Station at 2 p.m. and stayed until 4.50 p.m. She made her statement to Det.-Sergt George Kirby of Devon C.I.D. who is in charge of the local investigation.

Where is Richard Swann?

She was wearing a light brown check costume and was stocking-less and hatless. Her solicitor accompanied her back to Seaton, eight miles away, where she posed for a newsreel camera crew in front of her bungalow in Burrow-road.

Public appeal

During her absence at Honiton, Feliks Marek, 32-year-old Polish ex-pilot, stayed behind at the bungalow. While she posed for the photographers at Burrow-road Mrs. Swann made a public appeal for her husband to return.

She said: "I have just come back from Honiton and on my solicitor's advice I have made a long statement to the police which I hope will clarify the whole matter.

"I am sure that if the police had not given all this publicity to the affair they could have contacted my husband earlier. I am sure my husband will turn up wherever he is.

"I appeal to my husband as a gentleman and a father to come forward at once and relieve me of this terrible worry."

When Mrs. Swann visited Honiton, a large crowd quickly gathered outside the police station and stood waiting until she drove away.

While she posed for the newsreel men at Seaton she was watched by neighbours and holiday-makers.

Hotels in Seaton and Honiton are booked up to capacity with the influx of newspapermen, photographers and photographic wiremen. This sudden influx clashed with the normal holiday-makers and the congestion in hotels was acute.

New line

Last night Devon C.I.D. reported that investigations, started a week ago in Devon and London, were still continuing, but had brought to light no information regarding Swann's whereabouts.

If Swann is not found in a few days however, a different line of enquiry may be undertaken. But no new

Mark Carlile

*enquiries are being undertaken immediately as a result
of Mrs. Swann's statement.*

*Mr. Ambrose Appelbe, who travelled down to Seaton
on Tuesday night, returned to London again last night.
Mrs. Swann showed Mr. Appelbe, who is also acting for
Feliks Marek, many old letters and documents which it
was thought might throw some light on Swann's
whereabouts.*

After reading the newspaper, Gran came back to
help us with our puzzle again. All three of us sat there
saying very little but gradually fitting the pieces
together. Noreen and I concentrated on the top half of
the puzzle and Gran the bottom with the meadow and
all the wildflowers. It was slowly coming together, and
as it progressed it became easier because there were
fewer pieces.

Dorothy came in and sank into the armchair and
closed her eyes. Another long day had tired her out.
There is no break for a farmer. Every day is a workday
even if you are sick because the cows must be milked
twice a day. She had no one to turn to for help but
Noreen and me.

Gran made Dorothy a pot of tea and put it on a
small table beside her chair.

"Off to bed you two, the puzzle will still be there
tomorrow."

We carried the board with the puzzle on it into the
sitting room and placed it on the floor beside the piano.
Then, after our trip to the outhouse, we went to bed.

Friday was always the best day at school because
the next day was Saturday and we did not have to get
up early.

When we came home from school, we both went
down the garden to Chuggy's run but it was quiet and
he was not in his little house. He was gone. We would
never see him, or be greeted by him again. A sad end to
our pet but he was never supposed to be a pet as
Dorothy had told us.

Where is Richard Swann?

We sat on the front step and Tinker came along the garden path from the yard and sat with us. We both patted him and you could see that he appreciated our company and the attention we gave him as he wagged his long shaggy tail furiously. He had obviously been out on the common chasing cows with Dorothy because he had sticky buds and bits of gorse stuck in his tail and long coat. We carefully pulled all the bits out except the sticky buds which were well and truly tangled in his tail. Noreen went in and got a pair of scissors and quickly cut them out of his tail.

Gran came out and said it was supper time so we went in and washed our hands and sat up at the table.

Gran had made potato cheese, sausages and fried eggs which I always enjoyed. Followed by blackberry and apple pie and hot custard with clotted cream for dessert. I finished first and went back for seconds.

"You'll get fat eating all that cream."

I didn't take any notice of Gran.

"I couldn't find Melody on the common today," Dorothy said. "Tinker eventually found her lying down behind some tall gorse bushes and chased her out of there. I hope she is not getting sick. It is unusual for her to not follow the rest of the cows. I will have to keep an eye on her."

Dorothy did not say anything about Chuggy; she probably thought the less said the better. After supper, she had a cup of tea and relaxed for a while listening to the six o'clock news and the Archers, and then went outside to do the milking. Noreen went out as well to give her mother a hand.

I helped Gran clear away the supper dishes and did the wiping for her as she washed.

Gran often told me stories about when she was a girl. In 1900, she was living in a large house called Trengwainton (in Madron near Penzance) Cornwall where her father, Frederick James Evans, was the bailiff to Squire Bolitho. It was not an easy life as she often worked long hours. In 1905, the family moved to

133

Mark Carlile

Butleigh Court on the outskirts of the village of Butleigh (near Glastonbury) in the county of Somerset where her father was bailiff to Neville Grenville.

When we finished the dishes, Gran got out my reading book and I sat beside her and read a chapter to her. She said my reading was improving but added that it was important for me to practice by myself. I very rarely did this unless it was to read about birds in my little bird book.

When Noreen came in, we got out the puzzle again and sat with it until it was finished. It was the biggest puzzle we had ever done and took us many hours to complete. We put it in the sitting room again to keep for a few days before breaking it up and packing it away.

The lamp in the dining room was getting really dull so Gran lit a candle and turned the lamp off. She unhooked the lamp from the ceiling chain and put it on the table. She had to wait for the lamp chimney to cool down before she could take it off to clean it, and to refill the lamp with oil. We sat there in the candle light and the light from the fire as Gran got the oil can from the scullery and a funnel to refill the lamp as soon as it had cooled off. She waited about fifteen minutes before taking off the chimney to give it a good wash in the scullery. I helped her refill the lamp with oil by holding the funnel as she carefully poured in the distinctive smelling oil. Gran could tell by the sound of the liquid when it was getting full and made sure she stopped before it ran over. I carefully lifted it up as Noreen, standing on a chair, hooked it up to its ceiling chain again. Gran stood on a chair and lit the wick and replaced the chimney. We had light again. It seemed really bright with the freshly cleaned chimney.

We didn't have school the next day, so we were allowed to stay up late. Gran made herself a pot of tea, and when she returned we played 'I spy' with her until Dorothy came in from milking.

"It was cold in the cowshed tonight," she said. "I think we will have frost by morning."

Where is Richard Swann?

She threw another log on the fire and stood with her back to the fireplace for a few minutes to warm up before sitting down to a mug of hot tea and a biscuit.

"That's better," she said as she moved close to the fire with her hands wrapped around the mug of hot tea. "I am finally starting to get warm."

Gran had found the Friday paper about the Swanns but had not read it yet. It was still on the front page of the Western Morning News.

Gran read it aloud as Dorothy drank her tea. Noreen and I sat in front of the fire listening to Gran as she read. It was only a short article with headlines that read:

MRS. SWANN IS CALLED TO LONDON

Message from her solicitor

Mrs. Kathleen Swann, of Burrow-road, Seaton, has been urgently called to London by her solicitor Mr. Ambrose Appelbe, who, it was reported last night, advised her to catch an early train from Seaton today.

Questioned last night about her intension to travel to London today, Mrs. Swann denied that she was going.

Mrs. Swann thinks that somewhere within a 60-mile radius of Seaton, her husband, Richard Rhodd Swann, the 64-year-old city merchant, who disappeared from Bucehayes Cottage, Stockland, in September, 1947, may be hiding in a country cottage.

When he paid his visits to her in March and April, she said, he always walked. As these visits were made at intervals of three to six days it is not likely that he came from any farther away.

It has been suggested that Swann owned another country cottage apart from Bucehayes and it is here that he may be living now.

Mark Carlile

'LOOKED PROSPEROUS'

Mrs. Swann thinks that when he disappeared in September, 1947, he had a large sum of ready money at his disposal, apart from his estate of about 4,000 Pounds.

She does not think that he is short of money now and says that when he visited her again, starting on February 16 this year, he always looked very prosperous.

Mrs. Swann has said that her husband often used to amuse himself by acting and striking poses. He possessed several wigs.

An old friend of Misses Ida and Gertrude Farran, who were the aunts of Richard Swann, told a 'Western Morning News' reporter yesterday that the missing man often went for walks of 20 miles or more.

POLICE TALKS POSTPONED

The special conference of senior police officers arranged for yesterday to discuss new moves in the enquiries into the disappearance of Swann, was postponed.

Postponement was due to the fact that Div. Det. Inspr. W. Green had further enquiries to make in the London area.

Following new enquiries on defined lines, Devon police expect to learn something of the movements of Swann.

Div. Det. Inspr. W. Green, of Scotland Yard, may come to Devon in the next few days.

He will also send a report on his investigations into business transactions of Mr. Swann before he disappeared and on the results of the examination of the merchant's apartment at Ruislip, Middlesex.

"That London solicitor must be costing Mrs. Swann a lot of money; I wonder where she is getting the money?" Gran asked.

Where is Richard Swann?

"Probably that 600 pounds she got from that transaction where they thought she forged Mr. Swann's signature. The police seem to be questioning her a lot. They probably think she had something to do with his disappearance. He may have done a lot of walking, but he never walked from or to Axminster station which is a lot less distance than Taunton where Mrs. Swann said he set out to walk to when he vanished," Dorothy replied.

"Mrs. Swann sent him a telegram to come and visit his two sons on the weekend he disappeared. It looks like it was a trick to get him to Bucehayes so that she and her Polish boyfriend could get rid of him," Gran added.

"Okay, you two, up 'Timber Hill' to bed," Gran said. "It is very late, and we'll be going to bed soon."

She often called the stairs 'Timber Hill'.

The clock on the mantel piece, which Gran opened and wound up with a key every day, indicated 9:45 so Noreen and I left for bed.

I thought about what Gran and Dorothy had said about Mrs. Swann as I lay in bed and drifted off to sleep.

We did not get up until nine thirty on Saturday morning. The sun was low in the sky. I could feel its warmth as it streamed through the window of the dining room lighting up the table, and through the door of the scullery. Gran cooked us scrambled eggs on toast for breakfast and put a tall glass of milk by the plate. I didn't dislike milk, but we had plenty, and Gran always reminded us that we had to get our calcium.

After breakfast I put on a warm coat and got my air rifle and went out the front door and down across the orchard to the lower field. Tinker must have heard me come out the door. He was by my side as I went down across the orchard. The grass was wet from an overnight frost which was melting in the morning sun. My Wellington boots kicked up the moisture as I made my way through the long grass of the orchard. There were no rabbits in the lower field as I approached the wooden gate and climbed over it. I made my way across the field to the woods beyond where I hoped to find pigeons or crows in the tall trees. Tinker had wandered off somewhere. He was no longer beside me as I slowly made my way through the thickets and fallen branches of trees. I came to a small stream and followed its bank for a while. Way off in the distance I could hear the faint 'Boom — Boom — Boom' of what I thought was a water pump. When Noreen and I were wandering the woods one day, I told her it was a dragon breathing. I don't think she believed me!

I stood still for a while listening for birds. Suddenly I heard the flap of wings as a large bird landed in the tree behind me. I slowly turned around to see if I could see it. I strained my eyes looking through the thick foliage for movement hardly daring to breathe. As I waited, I caught the movement of a large black bird through the leaves. I aimed my rifle towards what looked like its head and gently squeezed the trigger. There was a sudden pop as the rifle discharged; I heard the pellet going through some leaves and a large black bird tumbled to the ground. I raced over to where it fell and could see that I had shot my first crow. I reloaded my rifle and continued along a path by the stream. If I went far enough, I knew I would come out at John Sangster's farm. Noreen and I had followed the stream before, back in the spring, so I knew where it would lead me. Tinker suddenly reappeared, and he looked a little wet on his legs and underbelly. He had probably crossed the stream or gone into the stream after a rat. I turned around and retraced my steps back along the stream and up the thickly wooded hill to a point where the woods joined the field above the farm. Tinker stayed with me all the way up the hill until we got to the top and then he wandered off again. I stood still as I reached a cow path through the trees and listened for any sign of birds. I couldn't hear anything except the occasional flutter of leaves when the wind blew in the treetops, and song birds chattering as they foraged in

Where is Richard Swann?

the fallen leaves looking for worms and grubs. I walked further along the path and stood still again but didn't see or hear any pigeons or crows. Way off in the distance I heard a wood pigeon cooing. I decided to return to the house as it was probably near lunchtime.

When I came out of the woods on the hill above the farm, I could see Dorothy in the yard working on the door of the cowshed. There was no sign of Tinker until I had walked down the hill to the water tank when he came racing down the hill to join me. Strange how he knew that I had left the woods and was on the way home.

Gran was laying the table for lunch when I walked in and slipped off my boots and put my rifle away.

During lunch, Dorothy reminded us that she was picking apples on Sunday and needed our help with the picking, sorting and packing. Gran would be busy for the next few days making jam, applesauce and pies and bottling apples to use up the bruised apples that had fallen. The bruised apples could not be kept because if packed with the good apples, they would make the good apples rot. Uncle Len often took some for Aunty Nancy to cook and make pies.

After lunch, Gran made a pot of tea and sat by the fire making out her grocery list. Dorothy had her usual cup of tea and a biscuit and sat with her feet up reading the article in Saturday newspaper about the Swanns.

At one thirty, Gran and Dorothy got ready to go to Stockland for groceries. Noreen and I changed out of our farm clothes, which weren't very clean, and into our Friday school clothes, which Gran had not yet washed, so that we could go with them.

Mrs. Clark had a bell attached to the front door of her grocery shop so that if she was in her back room she would know when a customer came into the shop.

The bell rang as we entered the shop and again when I closed the door. Mrs. Clark was behind the big wooden counter opening boxes of canned beans and packing them on a shelf.

Mark Carlile

As Gran and Dorothy went through the grocery list, Noreen and I stared at the jars of sweets on the shelf behind the counter deciding on which one we would have. Mrs. Clark packed our groceries into cardboard boxes as Gran went through the list. When it was time to pay, I asked, "Can we have some sweets?" "Alright," Gran said. "What do you want?" We chose our sweets. Mrs. Clark weighed them out with her scales and put them in little white bags which she handed to us.

I helped Dorothy to carry the grocery boxes up to the car and put them into the back seat. Before driving home, we went in to see Aunty Nancy who lived in a house next to Mrs. Clark's shop. Aunty Nancy was busy making a wedding dress for someone when we arrived. The lady was coming for a fitting at four thirty. Nancy had been a dressmaker for a long time. Everyone in the village knew her, and as a result she was always kept very busy. Uncle Len came in when we were there so Dorothy asked him if he was still able to come and help with the apple picking tomorrow. He said he could and would be there at ten in the morning. We did not stay long because Aunty Nancy could not stop to talk; she just kept working while we talked to her. We said goodbye as we did not want to hold her up, and we showed ourselves out.

When we returned home, we helped Gran pack away the groceries in the scullery. Then I sat by the fire until supper time reading my bird book. I was still collecting birds' eggs, but now that I had most of the common ones, it was getting difficult to find eggs that I did not have. I did not have a rook's egg but there were no rookeries on our farm so it would be very difficult to get one. Rooks' nests are generally high up in large trees. There was a rookery in the tall trees opposite Stockland School. They were very noisy birds, always squawking and flying around. I was still looking for a curlew's nest but it was too late in the season to find any eggs now. I would have to start again in the spring.

Where is Richard Swann?

Noreen laid the table for supper while Gran cooked the shepherd's pie and vegetables. She was also making custard for dessert.

"Where did you go this morning?" Gran asked as we sat down for supper.

"I went out in the woods with my rifle and shot a crow."

"Poor thing," Dorothy said.

She did not like me shooting anything but was always appreciative when John Sangster came by with a rabbit or two that he shot for us.

I went back for a second helping of the shepherd's pie but did not have more vegetables.

"I don't know where you put it all, you must have hollow legs. You need to eat more slowly; you will get indigestion eating so quickly," Gran remarked.

She was always telling me that. I did not know what indigestion was so assumed I did not get it.

"Tinker was in a bit of a mess this morning," Dorothy said. "I don't know where he had been."

"He was with me in the woods," I replied. "I think he went in the stream after something."

"I wondered how he got so dirty."

After supper I got out a book that Gran gave me for Christmas. It showed all the countries in the world along with a little information about each one. It gave population, the country's flag, its location in the world and a few other principle details like what it produced. I sat by the fire flipping through the pages reading the information about each country. I liked geography and knew where a lot of the countries were. I had a stamp collection that I had been working on for a few years. Every time I got a stamp from somewhere else in the world, I would look up the country with the help of my geography books and Gran.

Noreen was helping Gran with the dishes and I decided to test her geographic knowledge when she had finished. When she returned to the dining room, I sat in a chair facing her asking questions about various countries. She had good geographic knowledge because she also liked geography at school.

"I have to test you," she said, "fair's fair."

I handed her the book, and she tested me until Gran came in with her cup of tea and sat in her armchair and started telling us about the copper mines in Cornwall. Then she told us stories about when she was younger. She lived in a big old house near Penzance, called Trengwainton, where she worked in a dairy making butter, cheese and clotted cream. She said that she and her sister had once seen a ghost in their bedroom. She was full of interesting stories about the rum smugglers in small Cornish fishing villages, and about how they brought in barrels of contraband rum from France into the rocky coves. She told us there is an inn on Bodmin Moor called the Jamaica Inn which is said to be haunted. Lots of travellers who have stopped at the inn have seen ghosts. It was built as a coaching inn back in the 1700s and was used as a staging post to change horses. Locals tell stories about how the inn got its name from smugglers, who smuggled rum into England from Jamaica and stored it at the desolate inn. Then, there were the Cornish wreckers, but that's a story for another day!

When Dorothy came in from milking, Gran picked up the Saturday paper and with her second cup of tea, started reading aloud the article about the missing Mr. Swann. The headlines read:

Important new evidence in Swann case

TODAY MAY DECIDE FRESH MOVES

MRS. CATHERINE SWANN, wife of the missing Ruislip tea merchant, Mr. Richard Rhodd Swann, returned to her Seaton home last night after a visit to her solicitor, Mr. Ambrose Applebe, in London.

Where is Richard Swann?

Unnoticed among the crowds at Waterloo Station, Mrs. Swann said before she left: "I came to see my solicitor regarding a new development. I have finished my business and now I am going home."

She had travelled to London alone from Seaton, and when she emerged smiling from the solicitor's office after half-an-hour's consultation she said: "I have discussed various aspects of my husband's disappearance with Mr. Applebe, but I can make no statement at present."

A conference about Mr. Swann's disappearance will be held in London today between Scotland Yard chiefs and the Chief Constable of Devon, (Lieut.-Col. R.R.M. Bacon), and other senior officers of Devon C.I.D.

YARD INQUIRIES

Fresh evidence which Scotland Yard are probing on behalf of the Devon Police is regarded as having an important bearing on the case, and the result of last night's work will be reviewed at the conference.

It may yield evidence sufficient to justify new and important moves, and may help materially in establishing Mr. Swann's actual movements after he set out on his walk to Taunton on September 28, 1947, from Bucehayes Cottage, Stockland.

Sightseers continued to visit the cottage yesterday. Again a police officer was on duty to protect the tenants, Mr. and Mrs. L.V. Hall and their family, from the inconvenience caused by visitors encroaching from the common onto the two acres of ground that go with the cottage.

At Mrs. Swann's bungalow in Burrow-road, Seaton, last night, Feliks Marek, her Polish friend, prepared supper for her return from London.

Mrs. Swann was taken by car from Axminster to Seaton, where she said that on the train journey she had found a note tucked into her coat.

It had apparently been left by an anonymous woman who sat beside her. It read: "Please tell Mrs. Swann that I admire her courage and wish her good luck and peace."

Mark Carlile

"That was probably a long and expensive trip to London and back to see her solicitor for a 30-minute meeting. And strange that woman leaving a note in her coat. I wonder if she made that up," Gran said.

While Gran was reading her newspaper, I got out my stamp collection. I had a few stamps that I could not identify as to which country they came from. The writing on them was not English, which made it very difficult to identify their country of origin. Two of them had upside down 've's', and other strange symbols that I did not recognize. I looked through all the countries that I had stamps for and noticed an upside down 've' on a stamp from Greece. That had to be it I thought, so I got two stamp hinges from the packet and stuck them in. I had a few others that had really strange writing but I just could not find what country they were from. I decided I would take them into school and see if my teacher could help me in our next Geography lesson.

Chapter 10

The Search Continues

When Dorothy came in from milking, Gran talked to her about apple picking the next day. Gran said she had lots of old newspapers to wrap each apple and it was something she could do to help.

"I can sit on a chair and wrap while the rest of you pick."

"Alright, Mother," Dorothy replied, "but I think Noreen should help you wrap, otherwise you won't be able to keep up."

"I'll help pick," I said. "I can go up the ladder. I like doing that."

I was not afraid of heights and could probably climb some of the trees that were easy to climb.

Gran said we could not stay up late as we had to be up early to get everything set up in the orchard ready for Uncle Len's arrival at ten.

"Off to bed with you now."

We did not argue. I packed away my stamp book and returned it to the bookshelf in the sitting room.

It had been a long day, and it took me no time at all to go to sleep.

The sun was shining on Sunday morning when Gran called us to get up. Fortunately, the weather was going to be kind to us. We sat at the dining room table waiting for Gran to bring in our breakfast. I could smell something cooking in the scullery and could hear sizzling. A few minutes later, she brought in two plates of fried eggs on fried bread along with a little bubble and squeak and a few mushrooms.

"Careful, it's very hot."

It was nine fifteen when Dorothy came in and asked us if we were ready to go to the orchard. She opened the orchard gate, drove the tractor through and hooked up the trailer that was parked up against the hedge.

"You two kids go and get all the cardboard boxes in the barn, also the pile of newspapers. Put it all in the back of the trailer."

While we did that, Dorothy got a can of TVO from a shed and fuelled the tractor. When all that was done, she asked us to help her get the ladder from the hay barn and load it on the tractor. Then she went in the house and got a wooden chair for Gran to sit on and put it on the trailer. Now that we had everything, Dorothy drove the tractor and trailer down through the orchard and stopped it by a tree that had cooking apples. We only had two trees with cooking apples so she decided to pick those first. Noreen organized the cardboard boxes in the trailer so that they would not be in the way of the ladder if we needed to stand the ladder on the trailer to get more height.

Gran came down just before ten, and Dorothy got her set up on her chair with a cardboard box and newspapers for wrapping.

Len arrived a few minutes past ten. We went around the tree picking all the apples on the lower branches that we could reach. When they were picked, Len put the ladder up against a sturdy branch and I went up and started picking. I had a little bag around my neck to put the apples in, and when it was full I came down and Len went up with his bag. I sat my bag on the ground next to Gran, for Gran and Noreen to started wrapping. When Len came down, he put the ladder up in a different spot and I went up again. While I was up the ladder picking, Dorothy and Len started picking the apples off the lower branches of the other tree. We had all the cookers picked by eleven-thirty and had started on the eating apples.

When it was twelve thirty, Gran said it was time for lunch. It was a beautiful morning, a perfect day for picking apples in the warmth of the September sun.

Gran had a stew for lunch which she had left simmering on the stove along with lots of bread for dipping and a potato salad. Everyone was really hungry. I knew Gran had made a trifle with cream for dessert so I did not go back for a second helping of stew. I did for the trifle though. We all sat and relaxed for a little while after lunch before going back down to the orchard to continue picking. We did not finish until just before five when Len left to cycle home. It was a long day for us all, but especially for Len as he had to cycle up from Stockland and back. He had been the village postman for many years and was accustomed to cycling every day, sometimes with a heavy load of letters and parcels.

We packed the full apple boxes in the barn, and Dorothy parked the trailer back by the hedge just outside the yard and unhitched it. It was almost five forty-five by the time we got in, and Gran was busy getting our supper ready. Noreen went into the scullery to help her while I laid the table. It was a long day but Gran never complained about work. Sometimes I would see her nodding off in her armchair if she was really tired, but not very often.

We finished off the stew for supper which Gran only had to heat up. There was trifle leftover from lunch because she had made extra.

We cleared away the dishes, and Noreen washed everything and I did the wiping to give Gran a break.

Later that evening, Gran filled the bathtub so that we could have a bath. Gran said we both smelled like apples and could not go to school on Monday like that. I went first, so I had the hottest water. After our bath, we put on clean pyjamas.

Gran said we could stay up for a little while but had to get an early night.

We both sat by the fire to warm up after being in the unheated sitting room for our baths, and Gran made us hot Ovaltine with milk. She said she would be very busy in the next few days cooking and bottling apples. She rummaged through the pile of papers beside her chair until she found Monday's paper with the Swann article. It was still making front page news.

"Off to bed with you as soon as you finish your Ovaltine and have been to the bottom of the garden."

We made our drink last as long as possible.

The headlines in large bold type read:

INTENSIVE POLICE SEARCH AT BUCEHAYES COTTAGE

Cordon around property: guard posted overnight

Shortly before 10 a.m. yesterday 25 police and C.I.D. officers of the Devon Constabulary, headed by Chief Constable (Lieut.-Col R.R.M. Bacon), arrived at Stockland, near Honiton, and cordoned off Bucehayes Cottage.

They immediately began to search outbuildings, the two acres of ground that go with the cottage, and also the surrounding land. This activity continued for over six hours.

It was after a visit to Bucehayes Cottage in September, 1947, that Richard Rhodd Swann, the 64-year-old city merchant was reported missing after setting out to walk to Taunton.

Police officers were posted at vantage points on the lonely common and moorland that surrounds the cottage, and no one was allowed to approach nearer than 200 yards.

The Search Continues

All day police moved about woodlands to the north-west of the cottage.

Uniformed officers who formed the cordon arrived in a police van, and altogether there were six police cars parked near the tall cherry tree that stands by the front door of the cottage.

Supt. W.C. Harvey, head of the Devon C.I.D., was present, as also were Supt. W. Johnson, of the Exmouth Division, and Det.-Sergt. G. Kirby of Honiton. The arrangements for the police cordon were made by Supt. Johnson. Some of the police officers were dressed in old civilian clothing and brought rubber boots with them.

Planes swoop

The actual search and investigations were conducted by senior C.I.D. officers, while Devon police provided a screen

The cottage, a poultry farm now occupied by Mr. L.V. Hall, who rents it from Mrs. Kathleen Swann, has at its rear a primrose studded bank, topped with a hawthorn hedge. There is a small orchard.

To the north, towards Taunton, is rough rising moorland covered with bracken. To the south, the land falls away to a valley, where there is a patch of reedy ground.

Shortly before 4 p.m., a twin engined taxi plane bearing Hendon markings flew in low and made several low sweeps, once coming down as low as 50 feet. The air taxi was followed by an Auster Moth, believed to have flown in from Exeter.

Sightseers were politely but firmly told that they could not approach and were moved on.

The Chief Constable left at lunch time. Supt. Johnson at 4.05 p.m., Supt. Harvey at 4.15 p.m., and the main body of police at 4.25 p.m.

Laboratory experts

One officer was left on duty at the cottage, and one at the end of the lane leading to it. No approach by unauthorised people was allowed.

Mark Carlile

It is understood that the police will resume apportions this morning.

Two experts from a forensic laboratory arrived in the morning and left late in the afternoon.

This new development swiftly followed the conference at Scotland Yard on Saturday, at which Col. Bacon and Supt. Harvey met Assistant Commissioner Ronald Howe, Commander Hugh Young, Supt. Peter Beverage, and Divisional Det.-Insp. Green, of Wembley, who is in charge of the London end of the inquiries.

"The whole circumstances of the disappearance of Mr. Swann were examined and discussed. It is not possible to give conclusions reached at the meeting at this stage of the inquiry," a Scotland Yard spokesman said on Saturday night.

Mrs. Kathleen Swann, the 37-year-old wife of Mr. Swann, spent yesterday quietly at her bungalow home in Burrow-road, Seaton, Devon.

When Dorothy came in from milking, and sat down to her cup of tea and biscuit by the fire, Gran said, "I have just finished reading the article in Monday's paper about Bucehayes Cottage. It said that 25 police officers were there on Sunday last, searching the common and all around the land that belongs to the cottage."

"Really," Dorothy exclaimed. "They must suspect that he was murdered by Mrs. Swann and that Polish friend who is living with her, and that he is buried somewhere around there. No other reason to conduct such a search."

"I expect they will eventually find him and those two will have to answer for it," Gran replied.

"It's hard to believe we may have had a murderer living just up the road from us," Dorothy commented.

"If she wasn't happy living with her husband, she could have had a divorce, but then she may not have gotten the house or any of his money. Perhaps that's why they murdered him," Gran suggested.

The Search Continues

Dorothy finishing her tea. "It's been a really long day and I am very tired," "I'm going to bed." "I won't be far behind you," Gran replied.

On Monday morning the weather was good, so we rode our bikes up to the Rising Sun to catch the school bus. I had several stamps from my collection safely in an envelope tucked in my shirt pocket as I was going to ask my Geography teacher if he could determine which countries they were from.

The weather was good all day, so after I finished my lunch of two cheese sandwiches and an apple that Gran had packed for me, I went outside to play football with some of my friends.

Right after lunch we had a history lesson, followed by a geography lesson. Halfway through the geography lesson when our teacher asked if we had any questions, I asked him about my stamps. He asked me to come up to his desk and to lay out the stamps on a sheet of paper. Then he asked the class to come up, one by one, to see if anyone in the class could identify where they were from. No one could. He gave us some work to do on a questionnaire and said while we were doing it, he would see if he could identify the stamps.

When we were finished, we had to pass our questionnaire to the person in front of us to mark as he read out the answers. I had gotten twenty-seven out of thirty correct when my questionnaire was handed back to me.

After the questionnaires were given back to the teacher, he said he had identified my stamps. He said three were from Russia, and two from Turkey. He said he could tell the Russian stamps by the architecture of the building, and the Turkish stamps by the wording on them, which was in Turkish. I thanked him for helping me and wrote an 'R' or a 'T' on the back of each stamp so that I would remember when I got home. On the way home on the school bus I took out my stamps and studied each one to see how my teacher had identified them. Noreen was sitting beside me and was now in a different class to me. I explained to her what I had done, and as I passed her each stamp to look at, she said, "Well, I wouldn't have been able to tell the way your teacher did, that's beyond me."

"Me also," I replied.

"We're starting to get ready for our Christmas play," Noreen said. "It is a long way off so we are just in the planning stage at the moment. Is your class doing anything?"

"They haven't said anything to us yet."

When we got off the bus at the Rising Sun, we got our bikes from the shed in the yard and cycled home along the old Roman road. A red tractor, pulling what looked like a large rake, came out of a farmer's field and advanced towards us. As the tractor got nearer we got off our bikes and stood at the side of the road to let the tractor and rake go past. The rake was so wide that it took up all the road. Had a car approached the tractor, it would have had to back up all the way until it found a field entrance to back into. As the tractor passed, the farmer waved to us and we both waved back. We had never seen the farmer before. Traffic on the old Roman road was minimal, but occasionally we would see a car or tractor, especially in the afternoon. Very rarely did we see any traffic in Post Lane.

I got out my stamp collection when we got home and stuck in the five stamps that my teacher had identified. All my stamps were now in my book. Sometimes I got stamps for my birthday or Christmas but did not get any for my birthday this year, except two stamps on a letter from my dad. Occasionally, Gran got letters from my dad in New Zealand and relatives in Australia, and I would get the stamps for my collection.

The dining room smelled of apples, and the smell was even stronger in the scullery. Gran had a big pot of apples on the stove, and screw-top jars on the counter. I had no idea what she was doing to the apples except that she was preserving the apples so they could be eaten next year or when she wanted to make pies. I had no interest in cooking because Gran did it all. She said she had been cooking and bottling apples all day, and probably would be for at least the next two days. I don't know how she managed to do all that and get supper ready at the same time.

"We need to take down our tent," I said to Noreen. "It has to be taken down and packed away before winter."

We hadn't used it for a long time. When we went out to look at it, the tent was sagging badly because all the guy ropes were slack. The ropes hadn't been tightened for several weeks. We couldn't take it down until the weekend because we needed Dorothy's help. We went around and tightened all the ropes and removed the few things we had inside and put them in the shed with the car. At least it wouldn't fall down if we had a strong wind. When we went back in the house, Gran was just laying the table for supper.

"What's for supper?" I asked.

"Chicken pie, mashed potatoes and carrots," she replied, "and bread and butter pudding for dessert."

I liked Gran's bread and butter pudding, especially with clotted cream which we often had available. During supper, I asked Dorothy if she could help us take down the tent on the weekend.

"I was wondering when you were going to take it down," Dorothy replied. "A strong wind would blow it over."

After supper, Gran went back to her bottling for an hour. When she was finished, Noreen helped her clear away the supper plates and cutlery, and wiped while Gran did the washing.

While Gran and Noreen were in the scullery, I sat by the fire in Dorothy's armchair thinking about various things. I often wondered if there was a murderer around here somewhere who would harm either Noreen or me. We did not like being on our own in the morning anymore when we pushed our bicycles up the steep hill in Post Lane just past the driveway to Snodwell. We often wondered if someone would come out of the common on either side of the road and chase us. It was a little scary. Going home we did not have those thoughts because we could peddle fast all the way down Post Lane. I started thinking about my air rifle and realized that I would not be able to shoot a rabbit because my rifle was not powerful enough unless I could get really close. I would have to be content with shooting crows or perhaps pigeons.

The fire was getting low, so I reached over to the log pile for another log. Gran kept a guard in front of the fireplace so I pulled it back and threw on a log. The fire was soon crackling again as the log started to burn. I warmed my hands in the heat from the flames and began to think of Christmas and what I would like this year. Noreen came in and sat in Gran's chair and warmed herself by the heat from the fire.

"I think we will get a frost tonight," she said. "I can see the window panes starting to mist up already and it is cold in the scullery. It will be cold cycling to school in the morning so we better wear our gloves."

After doing the dishes, Gran did a little more work on preserving the apples, and then came in and sat by the fire.

"Next year during the summer holidays, you should think about going to see your Gran and Grandpa on your mother's side of the family," Gran said.

"Where do they live?" I asked.

"They live in Bexhill-on-Sea in Sussex. I know they would love to see you, and Noreen could go with you."

"How would we get there?"

"Dorothy would take you to Taunton, and then you could catch the train," she replied.

"They would take you around and show you where your mother and father lived, and where your mother is buried, and I expect they would take you to see your relatives on your mother's side of the family. Your Uncle Gerald, who is your mother's brother, and Aunty

Patricia live in Bexhill, and I am sure they would show you around as well. Your uncle is a baker."

I was not thrilled about it, especially about the train journey. "I'll have to think about it."

"After Christmas, I will write to Mrs. Vile, and see if she would like to see you in the summer," Gran said.

We sat talking for a little while longer as Gran told me about my relatives in Sussex and Kent, and about where the Coates family lived in Fairlight. Once Gran started on stories about the past, she would often go on for quite a while. I did not know the places she talked about but sometimes she would get out an old photo album and show us pictures of the people and places.

"It's time for you two to go to bed. It's another school day tomorrow, so off you go."

It had been another long day for Gran because of all the extra work of preserving the apples, but it was nearly finished. She made herself a cup of tea and sat in her armchair with her eyes closed, unwinding for a little while and thinking of a more relaxing day when all this extra work would be finished. She was glad it only happened once a year. She opened her eyes, took a few sips of her steaming hot tea and read the article about the Swann case in Tuesday's paper.

The headlines, still on the front page, read:

Police call off Bucehayes Cottage search

LABORATORY TEST RESULTS AWAITED

Devon C.I.D. last night decided to postpone further search operations at Bucehayes Cottage, Stockland, pending the results of laboratory tests on certain articles removed on Sunday, and police guards were withdrawn.

Supt. W.C. Harvey, Chief of Devon C.I.D., said last night after the second day's search of the cottage, that there has been no developments.

It was from Bucehayes Cottage that Richard Rhodd Swann, 64-year-old City merchant, was reported missing after setting out for a walk to Taunton on September 28, 1947.

PIT DRAINED

Yesterday police attention switched from around the two remaining walls of an old outhouse from which specimens of earth and other objects were removed on Sunday to a cesspit which stands near the orchard at the rear of the house. The cesspit was drained and the contents closely examined.

Neither the Chief Constable of Devon, Lieut.-Col. R.R.M. Bacon, who had personally directed the search on Sunday, nor Supt. W. C. Harvey, were present yesterday, and operations were supervised by Inspr. W. Raymond and Det.-Sergt. G. Kirby of Honiton.

The overnight guard on the cottage had been reinforced by about 15 police and C.I.D. officers yesterday morning and a cordon re-formed. Despite intermittent showers, work continued throughout the day on the soggy ground.

POLICE REINFORCEMENTS

The surrounds of the cottage were as closely guarded as on Sunday and police reinforcements had been drawn upon from a wide area in the Honiton district.

The tenants of Bucehayes, Mr. and Mrs. L.V. Hall, who were renting it from 37-year-old Mrs. Kathleen Swann, of Burrow-road, Seaton, wife of the missing man, carried on their business as well as possible, and Mrs. Hall was seen to emerge at regular intervals to feed the chickens.

The Halls were the only people, apart from the police, who were allowed to move freely about the cordoned-off area.

Gran was sitting in her armchair fast asleep with the newspaper in her lap when Dorothy came in from milking. Dorothy did not disturb her and went back into the scullery to make herself a fresh pot of tea. When she went back into the dining room with her tea and biscuit, Gran was still asleep. As she drank her tea and dunked her biscuit in the tea, Gran suddenly awoke.

"Goodness," she exclaimed, "how long have you been in? I must have fallen asleep."

"I've only just come in. I made myself some tea and then you woke up."

"I must be really tired, it's been a long day. I don't normally get that tired. Good job you weren't a burglar."

"I've just been reading about the police search of Bucehayes. They had fifteen policemen guarding the place, and they drained the cesspit and went through the contents. What an awful job!"

"They must suspect she buried her husband somewhere there," Dorothy replied. "Why else would they do all that? It's really awful, isn't it?"

Gran handed her the paper.

"It's on the front page, right at the top of the third column if you want to read it."

Dorothy read the short article as she drank her tea. "Looks like they've called off the search for now, probably done as much as they could. It will be interesting to see if they find anything. I hope they didn't bury him on our common somewhere. That common the kids walk across from Boilen's down to Gypsy Manley's place is right behind the Bucehayes Cottage. He could be buried there as well, and it's a large common."

"I'm going to bed," Gran said.

"I won't be far behind you," Dorothy replied.

"Don't forget to turn the lamp out when you come." That was generally Gran's job as she was normally last to bed.

"I won't, Mother, good night."

Wednesday was overcast, but it was not raining so we rode our bikes up to the Rising Sun. If it was raining when we came home, which it looked like it could be, Dorothy would meet the bus so that we didn't have to cycle home in the wet. As we passed Gypsy Manley's place, he was near his gate trimming the grass. He waved and said "Good morning kids" as we slowly peddled up the hill. We waved back and wished him good morning. We didn't often see him, especially this early in the morning.

When we came home, it was raining hard as we stepped off the school bus but Dorothy was not there to meet us with the car. We didn't have raincoats, so we made a dash for the open door of the shed where we kept our bikes. Dorothy always said 'wait' if she wasn't there on time and it was raining, as she could have gotten held up for some reason. We couldn't see all the road from the shed but would be able to hear a car coming. It was a little windy, and as the wind gusts came the rain appeared to be coming down sideways.

The old Roman road is shown as 'Stockland Hill' on a map and runs along the crest of a hill with steep valleys on each side. It is windswept because there is nothing to break the wind. We stood in the doorway of the shed watching the rain falling and dripping off the roof and listening for a car coming. Where it dripped off the roof, it was forming a pool of water on the ground in front of the doorway. It was cold in the doorway and we were already a bit wet. We stood there waiting and wondering.

"I wonder if she forgot, or if it is not raining at the farm," I said to Noreen.

"She has probably just been delayed," Noreen replied. "Mum normally gets the cows in about this time so perhaps she had difficulty finding one in the rain."

Just then, we heard the sound of an engine and peered out the door to see if it was our Rover. It wasn't, it was just a car going in the other direction in a mist of spray as it sped past.

"Do you think we should cycle home?" I asked Noreen.

"No, Mum will be here in a minute. She will, you'll see."

The Search Continues

A few minutes later we heard the sound of a car again. As we looked around the side of the shed doorway towards the road, we saw the black Rover appear and stop. We jumped the rain puddle in the doorway and dashed out to the car and got in.

"Sorry I'm late. One of the cows got caught in some wire netting as I brought them in for milking. It took me a while to get her free."

"We were wondering what had happened," Noreen replied.

We were now a little wetter. The rain had made my hair quite wet, and moisture was running down my face, and my trousers were damp. Noreen's skirt looked wet, and her legs were wet and a little blue from the cold. When we arrived home, we quickly ran through the rain again getting even wetter.

When Gran saw us she exclaimed, "Go and take those wet clothes off before you catch your death."

She got us each a towel and clean clothes so that we could get out of our wet things and dry ourselves. We were both quite cold but quickly warmed up by the fire as Gran got the supper ready.

After supper, Gran suggested that I should write a letter to my dad. She said she would help me with it after she finished washing the dishes. I didn't like writing letters so hardly ever wrote one unless Gran suggested it. My writing was alright, but my spelling was terrible. It generally took me a long time to write a letter because of my spelling. I sat by the fire thinking what I would tell my dad until Gran came in with a cup of tea and sat by the fire.

"I'll get the writing paper and pen when I've finished my tea, and then we can sit at the table and you can write to your dad."

"All right," I replied. "I have just been thinking of things I can tell him. Where is he living in New Zealand?"

"He's in a place called Havelock North, a suburb of Hastings, in the North Island's Hawkes Bay area. That's all I know about it. He's working as a carpenter, and I believe he's building his own house. He sent me a picture of his house with his last letter. I'll get it and show you when you start your letter."

When Gran finished her tea, we sat down at the table and I started to write. 'Dear Dad' "Now what?" I asked.

"Well, ask him if he is keeping well, and tell him about some of the things you have been doing. He would be interested in that."

It was a struggle for me, but after asking Gran how to spell many of the words, and what things I could tell him, and when to put a comma or a full stop, I finally got it done. I was glad when it was finished. It took me a long time.

Gran put it in an envelope and addressed it ready for posting.

Gran got the photo of the house my dad built and handed it to me. His house looked really nice. It had a very large front garden with a revolving clothesline. The house was painted white with a veranda at the front.

"Did my dad get shot in the war?" I asked.

"No, he didn't," Gran replied. "He was one of the lucky ones."

"What did he do in the army?" I asked.

"He was a Military Policeman and served in France at the start of the war."

"Tell me about it."

"I'll tell you what I can remember of your dad's first assignment in France."

"The Army made him corporal (acting unpaid) and with his section of men, they boarded a train to Portsmouth then a troopship to France. He said it was the most frightening sea trip of his life in the roughest sea he had ever seen. They arrived in Cherbourg in the early hours of the morning. He said that most of his section were ill on the way over. They made camp on the sand dunes of Pornichet, a resort on the west coast of France not very far from Saint-Nazaire, but far enough to keep them out of trouble with the local people. At this point he was informed that he was only an acting corporal for the purpose of bringing his unit across from England. He was demoted and stripped of his stripes, in other words he had been used for free. A corporal is normally paid more."

"The army made him a Military Policeman because at the time there had been many undercover German agents in the Brittany area of France, and the army was engaged in investigating their whereabouts. They sometimes used civilian clothes and went into many areas of France. At times it was quite dangerous work, but he found it most interesting, and they did locate a number of operators. They were quite inexperienced for the work, but with the help of professional policemen, some from Scotland Yard, they made the grade. Later, when he was in India, he was awarded a Commendation for the work."

"His Duty took him across France (North, South, East and West). He said it was quite an exciting assignment until they suddenly found themselves being driven by the German Army towards destruction at Dunkirk. However, he managed to escape the main thrust and headed to Brest. They had no transport and found that the German Army had headed them off and were in possession of the Naval Base at Brest. They were then forced to head south towards the port of Saint-Nazaire."

"During their trek south across France, they arrived at the main railway junction at Rennes where they, along with a huge crowd that had gathered tried to get transport to the south. At the time they were not very popular with the French and he said they nearly got lynched by the crowd. They were travelling in a party of seven and were having great difficulty getting food and drinking water. The only water the French would give them was the slops saying that was good enough for them, calling them traitors for pulling out of France and leaving them to fight the German Army on their own. Which of course was true, he admitted."

I was listening intently as Gran told the story as I had not heard it before and did nothing to interrupt her.

Gran continued, "One of their party got blind drunk on some wine that he'd found, and when he saw a British Army Truck being driven by a Frenchman, he pulled out his pistol and threatened to shoot him, calling him a fifth columnist. The crowd in one mass turned on him and were after his blood. They ran down the street with the mob behind them gathering momentum all the time. At that moment, they saw a private car coming up the road towards them. When the driver saw the angry mob heading straight for them, he did a quick U-turn enabling them to catch up with the car. They jumped into the car and made their escape, virtually saving their lives."

"They progressed from Rennes to Saint-Nazaire and arrived there about three days later. He said it was a real shambles. They could not get within five miles of the port due to vehicles of every type being piled up, one against the other, packed up tight. You could not drive anywhere. They finally made it to the dock where there were queues of men waiting four abreast to get on the boats. There was one big luxury British Cunard liner, which he thought was the Lancastria. They tried to get on but were forced off by armed guards. The ship was full so it would have been dangerous to let more men on. That ship finally sailed at 3 p.m. that day. They watched her sail from the dock and when she was just about in mid-stream, a lone German plane approached out of the sky and dropped bombs on her. Three direct hits caused the ship to list, and then she rolled over and virtually within minutes she sank with thousands of men scrambling in the water. Whilst the sea was not rough, thousands lost their lives. They finally got on a small troop ship. About five thousand troops were really packed in; there was no room anywhere. He said that when they finally sailed out into the Atlantic Ocean, it was a broad moonlit night — a sitting target for planes or subs. They had to maintain complete silence to prevent subs from picking up noise. It was the most crowded ship he had ever been on. They lived on the ship's hard biscuits for days and smoking was forbidden. They finally made it to Plymouth Hoe. At the time, when they could just see land on the horizen, a group of Spitfire fighter planes zoomed down on them and demanded they identify themselves. To begin with, they thought they were Nazis. He said they gave them the biggest cheer you have ever heard and left them in no doubt. They had been boxed up for four days and nights with only whispers of sound."

"So my dad was like a secret agent in France, hunting down enemy agents," I remarked.

"I suppose he was for a while, but later in the war he was transferred to India which I know little about."

"Look at the time, it is way past your bedtime. Go down the garden and go straight to bed when you come back."

We put on our boots, Macks and a hat because it was still raining and blowing outside. Noreen grabbed the torch off the window seat and we made our way down the garden path to the outhouse. It was a nasty, blowy night and very dark. Noreen went in first with the torch while I stood outside. I felt cold standing there as water dripped off my hat and hit my face when the wind blew. It was a pitch black night but gradually my eyes became accustomed to the dark and I could see a little of my surroundings. When Noreen came out, I went in with the flashlight. It did not take me long to pee, and I was back out of the spider-infested outhouse. I hated going down there in the cold, dark and rain but Gran made sure we did it every night before bedtime. When we returned to the dining room, we took off our boots by the door and hung our wet Macks over the back of a chair to dry. Then we sat by the fire to warm up for a few minutes until Gran reminded us to go to bed.

Gran put down her knitting and reached for a newspaper to read about our missing neighbour as we left the warm dining room and went upstairs to our cold unheated bedrooms.

It was just a short article in Wednesday's paper with headlines that read:

POLICE LIFT BUCEHAYES CORDON AFTER LABORATORY TESTS

After a 13-hour search on Sunday and Monday at Bucehayes Cottage, Stockland, from which Richard Rhodd Swann, 64-year-old City merchant, was reported missing in 1947, Dr. H.S. Holden, of the Metropolitan Police Laboratory, yesterday examined samples of earth and other objects taken from there by Devon C.I.D.

Further consultations are expected shortly between Scotland Yard and the Devon C.I.D., during which Dr. Holden's report, which it is understood will be submitted within the next few days, will be considered.

Close secrecy is still being maintained by the police regarding the exact nature of the search operations at Bucehayes Cottage, but the guard was removed yesterday and the tenants Mr. and Mrs. L.V. Hall, and their family were able to resume their normal activities.

The police cordon which surrounded the cottage on Sunday and Monday was so tight that not even personal friends of the Halls were allowed to approach the house.

Police activities during the two days appeared to be concentrated in four places — an old outhouse, a duck run, a cesspit and a spot in the orchard which was left covered with a tarpaulin and corrugated iron sheets.

Police worked with buckets alongside forensic laboratory specialists and a number of bags containing samples of earth was taken away.

The Search Continues

Supt. W.C. Harvey, who is in charge of the local investigation, left his headquarters at Exeter early yesterday morning and had not returned late last night. Devon C.I.D. declined to comment on his movements.

Yesterday afternoon Mrs. Kathleen Swann, of Burrow-road, Seaton, wife of the missing man, took advantage of the fine weather and left her bungalow for a walk along the promenade.

Dorothy came in from milking as Gran was reading the article and sat by the fire to warm up.

"It was cold out there tonight, and I had a problem with one of the Tilley lanterns, I had to change the mantle. Then Melody nearly kicked over a bucket of milk. I just managed to catch it in time. I don't know what's wrong with her, she doesn't normally kick."

When Gran finished reading the short article she went into the scullery and made Dorothy a fresh cup of tea. Dorothy sat by the fire sipping her hot tea and dunking her biscuit in it.

"It is still raining and blowing hard, and the cold breezes coming into the cow stalls may have been what was upsetting Melody. That, as well as the noise of the rain on the tin roof. She probably didn't like it."

"Animals can be a bit finicky at times. You know how little things upset the horses at Fairlight when you had the riding stables," Gran said.

"I have just finished reading the article about Swann. Nothing much new in Wednesday's paper. They are just analyzing samples of dirt and other articles taken from the cottage. Also, the police cordon has been removed."

"I don't think they will find anything," Dorothy replied. "Mrs. Swann and her Polish friend are far too smart to leave any evidence. They probably buried him somewhere far from here, and he'll never be found."

"There are lots of commons around here, including our own, which would be very difficult to search. They could have sunk him in that bog near the house, in which case they will never find him," Gran replied.

Gran and Dorothy sat there in silence for a little while listening to the crackling of the fire as Gran poked it with a poker to get a little more life out of it before going to bed.

"I hope the weather is better in the morning," Dorothy remarked. "I am tired of all this rain."

The following morning the wind was still blowing a little, but it wasn't raining. After breakfast, Gran gave us our lunch bags.

"You have one dripping sandwich each, two cheese sandwiches and an apple. Make sure you eat it all, you don't want to waste good food."

"Alright Gran," I replied.

We walked to the Rising Sun to catch the school bus that morning and almost missed it. We were quite a way from the bus stop when we saw the bus arrive so we started running as fast as we could. We were lucky that the bus driver saw us running and waited.

As we got on the bus panting and puffing from our run, the driver said, "You are lucky I saw you. I was just about to pull away when I looked down the road and saw you running."

We flopped down in a seat at the back and soon regained our breath.

"That was lucky," Noreen remarked. "We nearly missed the bus. Gran and Mum would have been annoyed if we missed it because my mum would have had to drive us to school."

That didn't happened very often, but we had missed the bus occasionally because we dawdled on our walk along the old Roman road.

We rode our bikes home that day because they had been left there from the previous rainy day when Dorothy picked us up. We were always quick getting home on our bikes because it was either flat or downhill all the way home. It was still a little windy, so it was not very warm as we cycled home. We rushed into the dining room as we entered the house, slipped off our shoes and sat by the fire to get some warmth. Gran had a good blazing fire going and the hot flames soon warmed us up.

"What's for supper," I shouted to Gran.

"Rabbit stew," she shouted back.

Not one of my favourites, but it was okay. We sat by the fire until Gran told us to sit up for supper.

Gran shouted out from the scullery door for Dorothy to come in for supper.

When Dorothy sat down at the table, she said she had difficulty finding the cows on the common.

"Thank goodness for Tinker, he saved me a lot of legwork tonight. He is a marvellous dog. I don't know what I would do without his help."

After supper we all sat by the fire for a little while as Gran and Dorothy listened to the news, followed by another episode of the Archers. When Dorothy went out to milk, I sat with my right ear up against the radio, listening to another episode of Dick Barton Special Agent.

When Gran finished washing the supper dishes and pans, she came and sat by the fire with her usual cup of steaming hot tea and started her knitting.

"We nearly missed the bus this morning," I told her.

"Why was that?" she asked.

"I don't know, perhaps we left late as we had to walk."

"I don't think so," Gran replied. "You must have dilly dallied on your walk, that's probably what made you late."

I couldn't argue with her as she was generally careful to ensure we left at the correct time. Later that evening, Noreen asked Gran if she knew anything about the riding stables that her mum had been involved with at Fairlight.

"Yes I do," Gran replied. "What do you want to know?"

"Anything about how it was started and who was running it."

She knew her Mother had been involved with it.

"Well, the riding stables started in the 1930s with all three sisters involved: your mother, Aunty Muriel and Aunty Nancy. They had about five horses and hired them out by the hour. They also gave riding lessons. It was a very profitable business. Your mother worked at it full-time. While Aunty Nancy was part of the business, she ran a dressmaking business as well. She was very clever and was in great demand. It was because of the riding school that your mother became associated with the author Catherine Cookson, and they became friends. Catherine loved horses and so they spent many hours together. Bernard, Michael's dad, did a lot with the horses but was never a really good rider."

"On one occasion, the riding school organized and ran an adventure holiday through the hills by way of the Cinque Ports, Hastings to Dover (on the white cliffs)."

"What are the Cinque Ports?" I asked.

"Originally they were a confederation of five harbours: Sandwich, Romney, Dover, Hythe and Hastings. They were grouped together for military and trade purposes."

"Michael's dad did not ride a horse but drove a support car and trailer with the camping equipment. He would set up the camp and get the tents pitched. The cook rode in the car with him. Bernard also helped with the cooking."

"The first time they did the trip, they got a lot of publicity. They followed the old stagecoach route and at every stop were met by reporters. Bernard said it was quite an exciting experience. They were helped by farmers on the route with feed and water for the horses. They also had two of Aunty Muriel's Dalmatian dogs with them, the ones with spots that she used to breed.

The Search Continues

They were beautiful animals. They all had their photo in most of the papers. "

Gran had a really good memory and could remember a lot about the riding school that her four children ran and loved to sit and tell us stories about the past.

We both sat and listened intently, and Noreen had many questions about her mother's riding business.

I got out my atlas and looked to see where Hastings was located, and the Cinque Ports, so that I could find the places the riding school visited on their adventure holiday. I showed Noreen where they rode on their trek across Sussex.

It was Friday so we could stay up late as we didn't have school the next day.

Gran got another cup of tea and came back and read the newspaper article about Bucehayes.

It was another short article with the following headlines:

POLICE AWAIT REPORT

BUCEHAYES QUIET

Devon C.I.D. has not yet received the report of Dr. H.S. Holden, of the Metropolitan Police Laboratory, who is examining samples of earth removed from Bucehayes Cottage, Stockland, on Sunday and Monday.

It was from Bucehayes Cottage that Richard Rhodd Swann, 64-year-old Ruislip merchant, was reported missing after setting out for a walk to Taunton, on September 28, 1947.

New police inquiries into his disappearance are not expected until this report is received. It is understood that it will be ready in a few days.

Police have not resumed operations at the cottage after the search was suddenly called off on Monday afternoon and yesterday afternoon the little whitewashed house was again standing in peaceful isolation.

Bucehayes Cottage is rented by Mr. and Mrs. L.V. Hall from Mrs. Kathleen Swann, of Burrow-road, Seaton, and wife of the missing man.

Gran put down the paper and sipped her tea.

"Anymore news about the missing man from up the road?" I asked.

"Not really," Gran replied. "The police are waiting on reports."

I got out a set of playing cards and we persuaded Gran to play with us. She threw another log on the dying fire and stoked the coals into life again.

Noreen and I often played cards but it was more fun when Gran played with us. She was good at card games and often beat us. It was more of a challenge when she played, and a lot more fun.

Dorothy came in from milking about eight thirty and Gran stopped playing to make her a fresh pot of tea.

"Gran has been telling us about the riding stables you had at Fairlight," Noreen said to her mother.

"Yes, those were good years. We had a good profitable business going. I loved working with the horses and teaching at the riding school."

"Why did you give it up?" Noreen asked.

"It was because of the war. We were right on the coast where the German fighters and bombers flew over to bomb London and many other cities in the north. Between September 1940 and May of 1941, the Germans bombed many British cities dropping tons of high explosives. Over a period of about eight months, London was bombed many, many times. When they were finished bombing, or if our fighter aircraft drove them off, they would drop any bombs they had left on their flight path back over England. We lived right on their flight path. We thought it was too dangerous to stay there, so we sold everything and moved to Devon. It was a big upheaval for all of us and we lost lots of money because of it. It was better than risking the possibility of a bomb dropping on our house and losing everything we had, and possibly our lives."

"What did you do with the horses?" Noreen asked.

"We were able to sell three to friends, and the other two we advertised in the Hastings Observer along with Muriel's Dalmatian dogs. All were sold."

"I hated to see my beautiful horses go. It almost broke my heart to get rid of such fine animals but we had to do it. In hindsight, we should have gone back into that business in Devon. It is much easier work than farming and has a lot less risk, and the hours of work are considerably less."

"Did you ever have any more horses?" Noreen asked.

"No, I didn't, except for an old cart horse at Cummings Farm. He was a big animal. We would give you and Michael rides around the yard on his back. Nancy would be on one side of him and me on the other to catch you in case you fell off his back. We would put Michael on one side and Nancy would catch him as he slid off the other side. It was quite funny. You were only about three or four years old at the time. We sold Cummings because Bernard was away in the army (although he did come home while we were still there), and Aunty Muriel was getting married. Nancy and I could not manage that big farm on our own. That was when we moved to Snodwell Farm."

We were intrigued with the stories and loved to learn about the family's past.

Gran shuffled through the newspapers again until she found the next article about the Swann saga. The articles, although still front page news, were getting shorter. The headlines read:

Mark Carlile

SWANN SEARCH

Devon police waiting for expert's report

Devon C.I.D. last night had nothing new to report in the case of Richard Rhodd Swann, the 64-year-old City merchant, who was reported missing after setting out for a walk from Bucehayes Cottage, Stockland, in 1947.

They have not yet received the report from Dr. S.H. Holden, of the Metropolitan Police Laboratory, on samples of earth removed from around the cottage on Sunday and Monday.

Mrs. Kathleen Swann, of Burrow-road, Seaton, the wife of the missing man, will shortly make another visit to London, it is understood, to see her solicitor, Mr. Ambrose Appelbe. She told 'The Western Morning News' last night that she thought there was a possibility that her husband might be on the continent.

Mrs. Swann has received messages of sympathy from all over the country.

"No more news on Richard Swann," Gran said to Dorothy. "They are still waiting on laboratory test reports. Now Mrs. Swann is saying her husband may be on the continent. Only the other day she said she thought he was living locally when he was visiting her. Her comments sound really fishy to me."

"Me too," Dorothy replied.

"We may go and see Aunty Muriel and Uncle Cecil on Sunday," Gran said to us. "If the weather is good, that is. It is too long a drive if it is pouring with rain."

"Oh, that's good," I replied. "We haven't been to see them for a long time. Where is it they live?"

"They live near the village of Rackenford, about six miles from Tiverton."

"How do we get there?" I asked.

"We will go to Honiton first, then take the A373 to Cullompton, and Tiverton Road to Tiverton. Then we take the Rackenford Road to Holmead Farm. It is about forty miles and takes a long time because of the twisty roads."

I got out one of our road maps that Dorothy kept tucked between the radio and the wall of our window seat. I spread it out on the table and looked to see if I could find our route. It look me a little while but I was able to find the towns and roads that Dorothy mentioned. Noreen came over to look, so I proudly pointed out the way we would be going.

"You two better go down the garden, it's getting late," Gran told us.

We could see it was late but hoped Gran wouldn't notice. Reluctantly we put on our boots and coats and made our way down the garden to the dark little outhouse. I stood listening to a distant owl somewhere in the woods, and the occasional bark of a fox. The outhouse door rattled and Noreen came out and handed me the torch for me to go inside. As we walked back up the garden, we heard two foxes barking in the distance.

"Did you hear that?" Noreen asked. "I hope they're not after our bantams."

"I think they're too far away."

When we returned to the dining room and stood by the fire to warm ourselves, Gran instructed, "Five minutes, and then off to bed."

On Saturday morning, we sat at the dining room table drinking the glass of milk that Gran had given us while she finished cooking our breakfast of poached eggs on toast and fried tomatoes. We both loved fried tomatoes for breakfast but only got them when Gran had tomatoes left over from the day before. After breakfast, we sat by the fire for a little while until Dorothy finished her milking and cleaning of the cow stalls, and came in for her morning cup of tea and biscuit.

Mark Carlile

"Can you help us take down the tent this morning?" Noreen asked her mother. "I expect it is dry because it doesn't look like it rained overnight, and if we go to Tiverton on Sunday, there won't be time to do it tomorrow."

"I'll help you just before lunch to make sure it's dry. We don't want to pack it away with any moisture on it because it will go mouldy over winter. You two kids take down as much as you can while it is still standing, and then I'll help you pack it away."

"Alright," Noreen replied.

Later that morning, we started to take the tent down. It was sagging badly again in spite of the fact that it was not long ago that we had tightened all the guy ropes. We decided that the ropes that had little or no tension on them could be released because they weren't supporting the tent. I got a cardboard box from the garage, then we released all the slack guy ropes and pulled out the tent pegs. When Dorothy came to help us, the tent was sagging and leaning badly. We released a few more guy ropes, and the tent started to fall. Dorothy caught the tent pole as it fell slowly into her outstretched hand, and she lowered it to the ground. It took us a little while to fold up the tent and pull the remaining pegs. Where the tent had been, there was a big round patch of brown grass because inside the tent the grass did not get any water or light.

The three of us carried the heavy canvas tent into the garage where it would stay until next spring.

After lunch, Gran made out her shopping list, making frequent trips to the cupboards in the scullery to see what she needed. Noreen and I changed out of our dirty clothes, and at two o'clock we drove into Stockland for grocery shopping at Mrs. Clark's.

Gran and Dorothy went down Gran's shopping list checking off each item as Mrs. Clark placed them in cardboard boxes on the counter. Gran had a long list this week because she was getting provisions for making her Christmas puddings and cake. Noreen and

The Search Continues

I leaned up against the tall wooden counter, picked out the sweets that we wanted, and looked around the shop for other things we could get Gran to buy.

"Can you buy some chocolate biscuits?" I asked Gran. "We never have those."

"Alright," Gran replied, "but don't expect them very often because they are expensive, and not good for your teeth." Gran always got the plain biscuits or digestive biscuits that we didn't like very much.

Gran bought the sweets that we wanted, Sherbet Lemons for Noreen, and Liquorice Allsorts for me.

After she paid, Noreen and I helped Dorothy to carry out the grocery boxes and load them in the car. Gran slipped in to see Aunty Nancy, to see if she had any more newspapers with articles about Bucehayes Cottage and the missing Mr. Swann.

We were sitting in the car with Dorothy, eating our sweets when Gran came back and said that there had been no more articles about Richard Swann. Just before we drove off, Uncle Len came along on his bicycle and chatted to Gran and Dorothy for a while. He said he was getting ready to make his cider which he made every year for himself and his friends. He had his own apple orchard at the rear of the church as well as a large vegetable garden and always had a good crop of cider apples. It was only a short visit because Dorothy wanted to get home to get the cows in before it started to get dark. We all said 'goodbye' and Dorothy drove home.

After we unloaded the groceries into the scullery, Dorothy and Noreen quickly changed into their old clothes and went up Post Lane to the common get the cows.

I helped Gran pack away the groceries and then went up the lane with a bucket of water and feed for the bantams. They must have been hungry because as I went through the gate, they all started clucking and came running towards me. I threw down their feed and filled the water trough and then went into their hutch to collect the eggs. There were a lot of eggs today which I carefully placed in their feed bucket. Just as I went out the gate, I saw a fox running along the tree line of the field and disappear into a clump of bushes. I wondered if they had a den near there as we often saw them at that location. I decided I would walk over there one day and have a look. It was starting to get dark which was the time we had often seen them. I heard Tinker barking and saw the cows coming down the lane followed by Noreen and her Mother. I waited in the gateway until the cows had passed and joined Noreen and Dorothy on the walk home.

"How many eggs?" Noreen asked. She peered into the feed bucket on my arm.

"Lots of eggs today," she remarked. "They must have had a peaceful night with nothing to bother them."

I gave Gran the eggs when I got home, and she washed them and put them away in the larder.

"Our bantams have been laying well."

I helped Gran lay the table for supper, and then sat by the fire staring at the hot burning logs enjoying the warmth and thinking about our trip to Holmead Farm to see Aunty Muriel, Uncle Cecil, and Gilda and Gary.

I liked car trips but often felt sick riding in a car, especially in the back on twisty roads. Sometimes, Dorothy would have to stop for me to get out and get some fresh air because I felt so sick. I was always glad when we got where we were going.

Dorothy and Noreen came in and washed their hands in the scullery before sitting down for supper.

"Looks like it will be a good day tomorrow. We can plan on going to see Muriel unless we get some unexpected bad weather," Dorothy said as we started supper.

"You two better have a bath tonight so that you can put on clean clothes tomorrow. You don't want dirty underwear in case we have an accident." Gran always said that. She had some funny and strange sayings.

The Search Continues

"Heaven forbid, Mother," Dorothy responded, "we're not going to have an accident."

"Well, you never know."

After supper, Dorothy had her cup of tea and listened to the Archers before going out to do the milking. Noreen and I went up the lane to lock the bantams away for the night. When we returned, Noreen got out the book she was reading, 'The Famous Five' by Enid Blyton. Her book title was 'Five on a Treasure Island', which she had been given as a birthday present. I sat by the fire for a while and then went out to talk to Gran and help her wipe the dishes.

"Why did my dad go to New Zealand?" I asked.

"It's a long story, Michael, and I will tell you one day when you are older and better able to understand."

"Do you know how my dad met my mum?" I asked.

"I do, but that's a story I will tell you when we have more time, but not tonight. So remind me again one evening."

After I finished wiping the dishes and not being able to get a story out of Gran, I joined Noreen by the fire. I sat there for a while warming my hands and wondering what I should do. I started thinking about how I could get rid of the foxes in the field where the bantam coop was. I couldn't shoot them because my gun wasn't powerful enough. Then I had an idea. If I could find their hole, I could block it up with them inside. But would they dig their way out again? It was worth a try.

Gran came in with her cup of tea, so I had to get out of her chair.

"I'm going to read the newspaper and then we'll get your baths done." Gran said.

Gran got a newspaper from the pile beside her chair and looked through the headlines on the front page until she found the last article she had about the missing Mr. Swann:

Mark Carlile

Mrs. Swann has written to Home Secretary

'END PERSECUTION BY POLICE'

The Home Secretary, Mrs. Chuter Ede, will receive a letter from Mrs. Kathleen Swann, of Burrow-road, Seaton, this morning, asking for an assurance that the "police persecution" of her should cease.

Mrs. Swann is the wife of 64-year-old Richard Rhodd Swann, City merchant, who was reported missing from Bucehayes Cottage, Stockland, near Honiton, in 1947.

It is four weeks today since Scotland Yard issued a photograph and description of Mr. Swann, and Devon C.I.D. yesterday said there were no developments in the search for the missing man.

In her letter, which was posted yesterday afternoon, Mrs. Swann says that when the police visited her on April 12 she asked them, as she knew her husband would come back, to promise her that there would be no publicity.

"Within two days," the letter continues, "Scotland Yard circulated a misleading description and an out-of-date photograph of my husband."

"FRONT PAGE NEWS"

"I then became front page news, and irrelevant details were splashed across the papers. Although the wounding effect of such statements is obvious, not one word of repudiation has come from the police. May I have an official assurance from yourself that this police persecution will now cease?"

"For nearly a month, it has surrounded myself and my household, causing mental suffering beyond belief."

"As the legal wife of a man whom the police say they are still seeking, surely I am entitled to official advice of their conclusions and the understanding that the search will cease to involve me personally in undesirable publicity?"

The Search Continues

'PRIVATE ANXIETY'

"I have given the police search every assistance in my power. How long must public curiosity continue to be fed on my private anxiety?"

"Finally, may I have an assurance that I am free to sell the shares which my husband transferred to me, and which were properly witnessed, or failing that assurance, a statement from you as to why it is not possible."

Mrs. Swann last night said she has had no word from her husband since he last visited her on April 9, 1949.

Gran relaxed the paper to her lap and picked up her tea cup and drank the remains in her cup while deep in thought.

"Alright you two, time to have your baths so that you're clean for tomorrow."

I got out the galvanized steel bathtub from behind the stairs where Gran kept it and placed it in the living room on the floor. There was a big black spider in the bathtub so I tipped it out and stamped my foot on it as it ran across the floor towards the shelter of a large couch.

Gran came in with the towels, flannel and soap, and placed them on a small stool which she put beside the tub.

"Help me with the water, please," she said. "The buckets are getting too heavy for me."

We went into the scullery and she drew a bucket of steaming hot water from the copper which I carried to the tub and emptied into it. I took in about five more buckets of hot water, and then one or two cold buckets of water until Gran said it was the correct temperature.

Noreen went first.

"Don't take too long," I reminded her, "or the water will be cold for me."

Mark Carlile

After our baths we sat by the fire in our pyjamas and dressing gowns to warm up from the unheated living room. We both helped Gran empty the bathtub, then moved back to the fireside again. I was glad we only did this once a week because before we went to bed we had to make a trip down the garden in our pajamas with a coat over the top. It was generally a cold drafty trip. At least it was not raining and blowing.

Gran made a pot of tea for Dorothy who would be coming in at any time now. Just as Gran sat down with a cup of fresh tea, Dorothy entered the scullery and washed her hands in the scullery sink.

After washing she came in, cup of tea in hand and sat down by the fire.

"Jinx kicked me tonight. On my leg fortunately, so my boot took some of the impact but I will probably have a bruise."

"Why do you think she did that?" Noreen asked.

"I don't know," Dorothy replied, "but for some reason she did not like me walking too close to her after she was milked."

Gran said we had to go to bed early because we had to be up in the morning ready to go as soon as Dorothy finished milking.

After our chilly trip down the garden, we warmed up by the fireside for a few minutes and then Gran reminded us that it was bedtime.

We got up at seven thirty in the morning as soon as Gran shouted up the stairs that breakfast was ready. She had cooked us fried eggs and sausages, with a little warmed-up potato left over from yesterday's supper. I sat there dipping my sausage in the egg yolk until I had eaten the sausage, wondering how far I would get on the trip before I would feel sick and have to stop and get out. I sprinkled some pepper and salt on the rest of the egg and potato, and it was all gone before Noreen had eaten half of hers. Gran came in with our glass of milk which she liked to see us drink most mornings at breakfast.

The Search Continues

We were ready to go long before Dorothy came in, and as we waited by the fireside, I looked at the road-map again to see our route.

After Dorothy had washed and changed, she took the road map from me and she and Gran packed a few things to take to Aunty Muriel's, which included one of Gran's apple and blackberry pies. When Dorothy was backing the car out, Tinker came running from the hay barn, where he slept, to see what was happening. He sat and watched as Dorothy backed into the laneway realizing that we were all leaving him again. As we drove down the lane, we watched him as he ran after the car barking, but he soon gave up and walked back home with his tail between his legs.

"Poor Tinker," Noreen said. "He doesn't understand why he can't come with us."

The lane dipped down into the valley just past the Bond's place, and we slowly drove through the shallow stream that always ran across the road. Then the lane climbed steeply uphill and past the Richards' farm, before twisting its way to the junction with Viney Lane where Dorothy made a left turn. It wasn't long before we came to the Old Chard Road and then to Honiton.

I followed the route in my head as Dorothy made the turns and talked to Gran and Noreen as I thought it would occupy my mind and keep it off the car sickness.

Dorothy turned onto the A373 at Honiton, which would take us to Cullompton. Not long after we left Honiton I started to feel sick.

"Please pull over as soon as you can, I'm feeling sick."

I had been sick in the car before so Dorothy knew she had to stop as soon as possible. She soon found a gateway to a field and pulled into the grassy entrance and turned off the engine. I threw the door open and leapt out not knowing if I would be sick or not. After standing there for a few minutes breathing the fresh air,

Mark Carlile

I started to feel better. Sometimes I only had to get in the car and I would feel sick without it even moving.

Gran changed places with me because if I was in the front seat it was not as bad. Dorothy backed out of the gateway and we were on our way again. I wound the window down a little to get some fresh air, and it helped as well.

When we got to Cullompton, Dorothy took the Tiverton Road, and it wasn't long before we were going through Tiverton and on to the Rackenford Road that would take us to Holmead Farm. The Rackenford Road was narrow, twisty and hilly. As Dorothy didn't know the road well she was driving a little slower than usual. Just before Calverleigh as we were going up a gentle hill, the car juddered and there was a grinding noise as the rear driver side of the car dropped suddenly. We came to an abrupt standstill.

"Oh, my goodness! What's happened?" Gran exclaimed, as Dorothy immediately turned off the engine, applied the handbrake and jumped out to see what was wrong.

She could not believe her eyes when she saw that the rear wheel was gone. As all this was happening, a car that was following, pulled in behind us and stopped. A portly man who looked like a farmer, judging by his dress, walked up to Dorothy as she stood looking at the car.

"I've been following you for a little while and noticed your rear wheel wobbling badly but I couldn't overtake to stop you and tell you. Your wheel is in the ditch back there. I'll go and get it for you."

Within a few minutes he came back rolling the wheel along the road and laid it up against the rear bumper of the Rover.

"Are you going anywhere near a phone?" Dorothy asked him. "I will need to call the R.A.C. for assistance."

Dorothy had been a member of the Royal Automobile Club for several years and never had to call them before.

The Search Continues

"I'm on my way home," the stranger said. "I have a farm just a mile or two up the road. If you give me your name and R.A.C. membership number, I'll call them as soon as I get home."

"Thank you for your help," Dorothy replied. "I really appreciate it."

We all sat in the car talking about what had happened and waited for the R.A.C. to arrive.

Noreen and I got out to have a look at the car sitting badly tilted to the right, with the right side sitting on the road. There was a big gouge in the road where the car had dragged on the road before coming to a stop. We got back in wondering if we would still be able to go to Aunty Muriel's. We didn't have long to wait before a little blue and white van with the R.A.C. badge on the side and top arrived from Tiverton.

"That was quick," Dorothy said to the stocky man in a blue uniform as she greeted him.

"It's a slow day, and I only had to come from our headquarters in Tiverton, so you were lucky. Now what seems to have happened here?"

"It looks like the wheel came off, I don't know why," Dorothy replied.

He checked Dorothy's R.A.C. Membership Card and then examined the wheel and where it had come off the car. He advised her that there was very little damage but it would be best to install the spare wheel and have the other one checked before using it again. He took out the spare wheel. After jacking the car up with a jack that he got from his van, along with a new set of wheel nuts from his van, he installed the spare wheel.

"The rim may be bent on the wheel that came off so make sure you get it checked as soon as possible," the R.A.C. man advised. "The wheel nuts must have worked themselves loose or someone did not tighten them properly for this to happen."

He checked the wheel nuts on all the other wheels but they were all on tight.

"I will have to charge you for the wheel nuts but other than that there will be no charge. You will get a bill in the post."

He asked Dorothy to drive up the hill a little way and back again to make sure everything was alright before leaving.

After he left, Dorothy found a farm entrance to turn the car around because the road was narrow and she was facing the wrong way. Then we continued on our way to Holmead Farm.

The laneway into Holmead Farm was rough with deep potholes filled with water from a recent rain. We bounced along the level part of the lane with Dorothy going very slowly as the lane made a sharp right bend down a steep hill. We came to a large barn and then dipped down another hill to the rear door of the farmhouse. Noreen and I helped Gran to carry the packages she had brought and Dorothy knocked on the back door and we all went inside.

Muriel was busy cooking lunch but came out to welcome us wiping her hands on the apron she had on. We all went into the kitchen which was very large with a log-burning Rayburn stove set in one wall. It was warm and cozy in the kitchen from the heat of the stove. Gran unwrapped the apple and blackberry pie and some jars of bottled apples which she gave to Muriel.

"Thanks Mum, but you didn't have to do that, you know. We'll have the pie at lunchtime as I can pop it in the oven to warm up. I have lots of clotted cream to go with it."

We all went into the huge sitting room where Muriel had a roaring log fire going in the open fireplace. Gilda and Gary came in just after we were seated and we sat talking for a while. Dorothy told Muriel about the wheel coming off the car and how lucky we were not to have done any serious damage.

Muriel, who was a really good cook, generally cooked a lot of food as she did not want anyone going away hungry. She soon returned to the kitchen to attend to the oven, and the pots on top of the stove.

Just before lunch Cecil came in and said hello and sat with us until Muriel called out that lunch was ready.

Muriel had cooked a pork roast with baked potatoes, brussels, peas and carrots; and she had a large gravy boat full of steaming hot gravy as well as a dish of apple sauce.

"Can I have a piece of crackling?" I asked, as Muriel sliced pork off the roast for me.

"Of course you can," she replied. "There's lots here."

After Muriel had carved pork for each of us, the dishes of vegetables were passed around. I piled my plate high and swamped it with gravy before making my assault on it. I finished in record time before anyone else. I didn't go back for seconds, except for another piece of crackling, as I had found out what Muriel had made for dessert. After we had all finished, and the plates were cleared away, Muriel opened the warmer on the Rayburn and brought out a rhubarb pie, and the apple and blackberry pie that Gran had brought.

"Which would you like?" she asked.

I had the rhubarb pie and then went back for a slice of Gran's apple and blackberry pie which I covered with runny cream as well as a generous helping of clotted cream. I loved cream with my dessert. Gran watched me doing this and shook her head and smiled.

"I don't know where you put it all," she said. "You'll get indigestion when you get older eating like that, you'll see."

After lunch, we went into the sitting room and Noreen and I sat on the floor in front of the fire and played a game of Snakes and Ladders with Gilda and Gary. Dorothy and Cecil talked about the farm, and Cecil said he was milking twenty-five cows now but he had a milking machine, otherwise he could never milk that many. Aunty Muriel got out a bottle of sherry from the sideboard and poured Dorothy, Cecil and herself a glass. Gran did not drink. Muriel said she was a member of the Women's Institute, and that they were putting on a play at Christmas which she had a part in. "You must come and see it."

Muriel invited us over to the farm for Christmas dinner which Dorothy and Gran accepted as long as there was no snow around.

"I've started rearing turkeys," Muriel said. "I'll be having one for dinner this Christmas. I've received lots of orders for Christmas turkeys so I will be very busy killing and plucking them just before the twenty-fifth."

Muriel made a big pot of tea for everyone and cocoa for Noreen and me. We stayed until three thirty when Dorothy said we should be leaving for home as she had to get back to get the cows in for milking. It was cozy and warm in front of the fire, and unfortunate that we had to go out and get in a cold car for the long trip home.

As Dorothy backed the car out to go up the lane, Muriel, Gary, Gilda and Cecil stood by the back door waving goodbye to us as we drove away.

We slowly bumped our way up the steep lane, then around the sharp bend to where the lane flattened out and eventually met the road. It was nice to be on the roadway again after all the jiggling, shaking and lurching up the long rough lane.

It didn't take us long to get to Tiverton, and then on the road to Cullompton and on to Honiton. Just before Honiton, I started to feel sick and Dorothy had to pull over into a lay-by which conveniently was at the appropriate place. I quickly jumped out, took some deep breaths of fresh air, and walked around a little until I felt the sickly feeling pass. I changed seats with Gran and we were soon on our way again. Dorothy never complained about having to stop and always pulled over as fast as possible.

"No wonder you feel sick," Gran said, "after all you ate for lunch."

The Search Continues

"It's not that, Gran, It's the bendy roads and constant movement from side to side that seems to do it."

"I know it is, Michael, I'm just teasing you about the huge lunch you ate. You probably won't want much for supper."

We were soon in Honiton and on the road home to Post Farm. When we arrived, Tinker came out barking to greet us from where he'd been sleeping in the garage. He wagged his tail furiously as Noreen made a fuss of him. He didn't like it when we left him and went away.

When we entered the house the fire was out, and the house was cold. Gran and I stuffed old newspapers in the fireplace along with some bits of kindling that Gran kept in a bin beside the fireplace. As Gran lit the paper the kindling started to burn. Gran quickly added a small dry log on top, and we soon had a fire going.

Noreen changed into her old clothes and went out to help her mother get the cows in from the lower field for milking. It was getting dark early now and in the twilight it is sometimes not easy to see the cows.

After Gran had the fire going, and the lamps lit, she started to make supper. She warmed up some potato and vegetable leftovers and cooked some fried eggs to have with it. None of us were really hungry after our large lunch at Holmead Farm, but very rarely did I leave anything on my plate. Gran always said that there were starving people in this world who would love to have what we have, so we shouldn't waste our food. I always remembered that.

Several weeks went by, and one night when Dorothy came in from milking and was sitting down by the fire chatting, Gran said it was strange that there had been no further news about the missing Richard Swann.

"I will be surprised if we hear anything further," Gran said. "I think the police could not find enough evidence at that cottage after all their searching to arrest Mrs. Swann and that Polish friend of hers. If he was still alive, someone would have seen him. He would have had to get money from a bank or from one of his accounts somewhere, and the police would have been able to track him. If he did walk to Taunton as Mrs. Swann claims and was knocked down by a car, they would have found him by now."

"It's very strange isn't it?" Dorothy replied. "He's probably buried somewhere around here where the police haven't looked yet."

On the 25th of April, 1949, Mrs. Swann made an appearance on the television appealing for her husband as a gentleman and a father to come forward at once, and save her from this dreadful worry.

Later, she made a second appeal saying that if the police had not given this matter the publicity they have done, she could have contacted her husband easily. She again appealed to her husband to please return. She added that she is sure her husband would return from wherever he is.

Chapter 11

Goodbye Post Farm

It was a Friday evening, and we didn't have to get up early in the morning, so I thought it a good time to ask Gran about how my dad became a carpenter. When Gran had finished her conversation with Dorothy, I asked her.

"Well, let me see what I can remember. He first started as a ladies' and men's hairdresser which we got him into. He worked at it for about a year. He did not really like hairdressing, and eventually the shop asked him to find another job. Then he got himself a job as a hotel lift boy, he was going to learn the hotel business. He didn't last very long at that because he ran afoul of an old lady and was sacked. Your grandad and I were very upset with him over that and were at a loss to know what to do next with Bernard. He told us that he wanted to be a carpenter. One of his sisters, I think it was Muriel, was the secretary to a builder, and he started work with that firm as an apprentice carpenter and joiner. He had to start work in the joiners shop first where he learnt how to use a mortising machine, but he really wanted to work with hand tools. He received his first pay packet of two shillings and sixpence after the first week and went out and purchased a new cap. The machine he was using threw wood chips all over the place and he said it was necessary to keep the wood chips out of his hair. He said that being an apprentice meant he was at everyone's beck and call, particularly the head machinist who was not the friendliest, especially to apprentices. On one occasion your dad fell out with him badly. As the head machinist passed by the machine your dad was using, he grabbed your dad's hat and wiped the bearings with it. The bearings were covered in thick black grease. Your dad saw red and picked up a length of wood and laid him out. He was so scared because he was a very mean man. He left work and came home and didn't go back until the next day. When he went back, all the people in the joiner's shop clubbed together to buy him a new hat which he was very grateful for. He said the head machinist threatened to kill him. He was in the joiners shop for about eighteen months where he learnt to use hand tools. He was then transferred to building sites. He loved that work very much and never looked back."

Dorothy was listening to Gran telling this story about my dad and said she remembered about the incident with his cap.

"Your dad was quite a good hairdresser you know. He often did Nancy, Muriel and my hair, and sometimes cut it as well, but it was not what he wanted to do. He wanted to be a carpenter, and loved that work, and was very good at it. I remember he once built a set of stairs for the house of author Catherine Cookson. It was a long curved flight of stairs that ran from her foyer to the upper level. Not easy to build. She was very pleased with his work."

"When we moved into Trengwainton (Mother called it Trengwainton after the name of the big house they had lived in, in Cornwall), your dad built dog kennels for us. We started boarding dogs as a business, and later, Muriel started breeding Dalmatians. Bernard was always building something for us when we lived at Trengwainton. He saved us a lot of money when we started the kennels and horse riding businesses. He loved doing anything with wood."

Goodbye Post Farm

I loved listening to the stories about my dad and always sat listening without interrupting Gran or Dorothy. Dorothy often told me that she was very close to my dad, probably because of their mutual involvement in the horse riding business.

I realized that the Second World War changed the lives of so many people and certainly changed the direction of the lives of all my immediate family. To uproot from their home (in such a beautiful part of the country according to Gran's description), to leave their two business ventures, to move to Devon where they knew no one, and to start farming must have been a considerable challenge.

I sat beside the fire pondering all this and wondered how they had the courage to take such drastic steps.

"Did you have to leave Trengwainton?" I asked.

"No, we didn't have to leave," Dorothy replied, "and it was a very difficult and costly decision. We realized that if we stayed we were not only risking all our lives, but everything we had if Trengwainton were to be hit by a stray German bomb. The risk was too great to stay."

It was getting late, and it wasn't long before Gran told us to make our trip down the garden and then to bed.

That night, when I was tucked up in bed listening to the wind rustling the leaves on the trees in the lane, I thought about the Second World War. How lucky my dad was to come back and start a new life and not be in an unmarked grave somewhere in Europe. I thought about the family's move to Devon and was thankful I was here as I slowly drifted off to sleep.

When I awoke, I put on my dressing gown and slippers and found Gran sitting at the dining room table drinking a cup of tea. She seemed deep in thought about something.

"What would you like for breakfast?"

"Scrambled eggs on toast," I replied, "with some bacon."

Mark Carlile

When Gran went into the scullery to make my breakfast, I looked out the window to see what the weather was doing. Low cloud hung over the valley, and a very fine rain was falling. There was still some wind as I could see the trees in the lane bending over occasionally with the wind gusts. Not very nice, and it looked like it was in for the day.

Noreen came into the dining room in her dressing gown and went into the scullery to ask Gran what was for breakfast.

"Michael's having scrambled eggs on toast and bacon. Do you want that as well?"

"Yes please, but no bacon," she replied, and came back into the dining room with two glasses of milk that Gran had poured for us.

After breakfast, we went out into the hay barn and played with Tinker for a while. It was such a cold miserable day that we soon went back inside to warm up by the fire.

Later, Noreen helped Gran make Christmas puddings. When I found out what they were making, I helped for a little while. It was always fun to help with the puddings because we could eat some of the sultanas and raisins that go into puddings. Gran always mixed silver sixpences into the puddings, which we hoped to find. It made us realize that Christmas was not too far away now. We often made our own Christmas chains out of strips of coloured shiny paper and hung the chains from the oil lamp over the dining room table to the four corners of the room.

Noreen had a part in the school play which we all went to see. She was really excited about playing the part of Madonna in the nativity scene. After the play ended, several scenes were set up again so that a photographer could take pictures for the newspaper, and for the actors to purchase.

That Christmas, we went to Holmead Farm to spend Christmas Day with Aunty Muriel, Uncle Cecil, Gilda and Gary. The weather was good, and this trip was

Goodbye Post Farm

uneventful except for me having to make my usual stops because of car sickness. Aunty Muriel had a huge turkey with all the trimmings for dinner, and Christmas pudding with clotted cream for dessert. Gran warned me about going back for seconds because Christmas puddings are very rich, but I did have a little slice.

It was a fun Christmas, but again, we had to leave for home early in the afternoon, because it got dark so early and Dorothy had to get the cows in for milking before dark.

The months sped by in the New Year, Noreen celebrated her eleventh birthday in February, and haymaking was soon upon us.

One evening, when Dorothy came in from milking and sat down to have her cup of tea and biscuit, Gran said that they had something they wanted to talk to us about. The first thing that came into my head was — 'What have I done now'.

"We are going to sell Post Farm," Gran said.

It came as a complete shock to Noreen and me, and we both tried to speak at once.

"Where are we going to go?" we both asked.

"Michael and I are going to go to Tiverton to live so that we are near Aunty Muriel," Gran replied.

"And Noreen and I will find somewhere to live in Stockland so that Noreen can go to the Honiton Secondary School. And we will be near Aunty Nancy," Dorothy said.

We had always lived in the same house and were more like brother and sister to each other than cousins.

Post Farm was sold in August of 1952, for 2,750 pounds.

It was a sad day when we left Post Farm. We had spent many happy and memorable years of our childhood there, and would now be starting a new chapter of our lives in new surroundings.

In 1960 newspapers reported:

Mark Carlile

Skeleton in Chains Mystery

London, January 5, 1960

Devon police were today awaiting a pathologist report on a skeleton in chains found in a sewage disposal pit at a disused army camp near Plymouth.

Police think that before the skeleton collapsed and crumbled it was held by the neck, the arms and legs to three padlocked chains hanging from brackets in the wall of the pit.

It is thought the skeleton may be that of the 64-year-old Richard Swann, a wealthy tea merchant, of Ruislip, near London, who disappeared in 1947 from a cottage about 50 miles from the pit in which the skeleton was found.

Police made long enquiries after his disappearance but failed to find any trace of him.

Last June his wife was given leave by the High Court to presume him dead and she remarried.

The camp was last used in 1946. The pit was covered with a concrete slab. There was clothing, including a pair of brown shoes, on the bones.

A cursory examination of the skeleton yesterday revealed no obvious signs of violence.

SKELETON FOUND IN SEWAGE PIT

Police Await Report

Exeter police yesterday talked with Mrs. Catherine Marek, former wife of Mr. Richard Rhodd Swann, a tea merchant of Ruislip, Middlesex, who disappeared in 1947. Her call was in connection with the finding of a skeleton chained in a sewage inspection pit in a disused Service camp near Plymouth on Saturday.

Goodbye Post Farm

"Mrs. Marek was unable to help us or we to help her," a police official said. "We are waiting for the pathologist's report, which we hope to get sometime tomorrow. We are hoping to get some useful information from it."

Mr. Swann, who was 64, visited his wife and their two sons at Bucehayes Cottage, Cotleigh, near Honiton, Devon, in September 1947, and on the afternoon of September 28 left the cottage to walk to Taunton. He was never seen again.

Police Check Chained Skeleton

Plymouth England, January 7, a skeleton found chained to the wall of a sewage inspection pit may be the remains of an American.

Police said this was among theories they were working on after discovering a pair of brown shoes with the pile of human bones.

The shoes were labeled "Grenadier Last" — the trademark of an American company. They also are manufactured in Britain but only for export.

A farmer grazing his cattle through the crumbling remains of an abandoned World War II naval base near here discovered the skeleton Monday. It was chained to the rungs of an iron ladder on the wall of a covered sewage pit.

Police pathologists are examining the bones at an Exeter hospital. They believe they had been in the pit about 10 years.

Fragments of the clothing, the brown shoes and a wallet containing a sodden red notebook have been sent to the forensic science laboratory in Bristol.

Scotland Yard is checking its files of missing persons for a clue to the skeleton's identity.

Mark Carlile

CHAINED SKELETON FOUND IN ENGLAND

PLYMOUTH, England —
A chained skeleton found at the bottom of a sewage pit was identified Thursday January 8 as the remains of a young Englishman who seemed to like shackling himself in strange locales.
The skeleton, police said, belonged to James Duncan Dunn, 23.
He disappeared in March 1958.
Just a month before his disappearance Dunn had been found chained to the railings of a house in London's sedate South Kensington district.
He was freed then by firemen.
Last Saturday, a farmer wandering across a now deserted World War II Naval base spotted Dunn's bones.
Three chains secured the skeleton to the rungs of an iron ladder.
Identification was made by Dunn's relatives, who recognized an inscribed watch.

There was never any more news about our neighbour, Richard Swann, and as far as we know he was never found.

Did Mrs. Swann and her Polish friend murder her husband and bury him on the common, or in the swamp near Bucehayes Cottage? We may never know the answer to that question — two people who are now deceased took the answer to their graves.

Epilogue

The writer contacted the Devon and Cornwall Police on September 3, 2015, asking if Richard Rodd Swann, who disappeared from Bucehayes Cottage, Post Lane, Cotleigh, Near Honiton, Devon, in September of 1947, was ever found.

Below is the reply I received:

A search was conducted on the Missing Persons database (Compact) and no records were found.

The Records Management Centre, a facility used to store more current or regularly reviewed case materials, was also consulted and they confirmed they held no information relating to this case.

Finally, the Heritage and Learning Resource Centre (HLRC) which is a department within Devon and Cornwall Police responsible for maintaining and developing the Force's historic collection were consulted.

The HLRC has a significant amount of information that is uncatalogued and a comprehensive searchable list of all the information that is stored does not exist.

A search of the electronically catalogued information has been conducted but no information relating to the case in question can be found.

Mark Carlile

Unfortunately, I am unable to confirm if Devon and Cornwall Police does hold any information regarding this missing person and the following explanation should assist as to why your request engages section 12(2) of the Freedom of Information Act 2000:

In order to establish if information is held it would be necessary to manually search through all the information held within the HLRC.

The HLRC have entered approximately 11,000 physical items onto the electronic system in the last 18 months from 2 rows of boxes in the storage area and there are at least another 5 rows to go plus another room.

Therefore to conduct the aforementioned searches would exceed the appropriate limit of 18 hours.

The time period of 18 hours is considered the 'appropriate limit', as per section 12(3), to the amount of time/money spent on one individual request under the Freedom of Information and Data Protection (Appropriate Limit and Fees) Regulations 2004.

I have a duty to advise and assist you on how your request could be refined, but unfortunately I am unable to identify how rewording your request would help us reduce the time it would take to search for the information that you are interested in.

The HLRC is working, through the help of volunteers, to get the information that they hold catalogued and organised into a workable order, but due to the volume of information that is held it is a slow process.

Epilogue

Should you have any further inquiries concerning this matter, please contact me quoting my reference number as above.

Yours sincerely

Freedom of Information Officer

Mark Carlile

Front cover picture. Post Farm
Rear cover picture. The lonely driveway into Bucehayes Cottage

57769715R00115

OKANAGAN REGIONAL LIBRARY
3 3132 03894 0385

Made in the USA
Charleston, SC
21 June 2016